ARROWS OF LIGHT

A Spiritual Diary

By Steven Charleston

RED MOON PUBLICATIONS
Oklahoma City, OK 73120

Cover Art by Suzanne Charleston, www.suzanneartist.com
Book Layout by Lana B. Callahan, www.lbsdesignstudio.com

Copyright © 2015 by Red Moon Publications

Library of Congress Catalog Card Number: 2015934718

ISBN 978-0-9851419-7-4

Printed in the United States of America

Dedication

To My Great Grandfather
Noel Thomas Holmes
Who Opened The Bible To Me
And A Great Deal More

PREFACE

In my Native American tradition, four is a sacred number. When they prayed, my ancestors always turned to face the Four Sacred Directions, the holy compass that indicated the presence of God in every corner of life. When all four directions have been acknowledged, then the person at prayer stands in a divine state of equilibrium, in harmony and balance with all of creation.

It is not surprising then that I celebrate this fourth book of my meditations. With it, the circle is complete. I began drawing that circle in 2011. Four friends (there is that number again) asked me to join them on Facebook, the global network for social media where people post photos, graphics, and their opinions on every subject under the sun. I did not know what to share, so I decided to simply write whatever came into my heart each morning after I prayed. All these years later I am still writing and now there are thousands of people who read my meditations.

This collection of them is for the year 2014. It is a spiritual diary of every daily meditation, except for Saturdays, the day when I invite members of my Facebook community to pray together. That community is now international and includes persons from…well, from all four sacred directions. They are from all faith traditions and cultures. They are as diverse as the human family can be, but by the grace of these small meditations, they gather each day in peace and hope: in that wonderful sense of harmony and balance that is so healing to the human heart. I invite you to discover that same centeredness in the pages that follow. ARROWS OF LIGHT is a place for you to be in the circle of your own faith. Each day it offers you a way to turn to face the different directions of your life. In these meditations you will find words that speak to your struggles and your strengths, to your quiet times and your celebrations, to what overshadows you and what lifts you up. There is no agenda here except for the prayers that you bring with you. This book is holy ground because it is where you stand right now.

ARROWS OF LIGHT (2014) now joins HOPE AS OLD AS FIRE (2011), CLOUD WALKING (2012), and CLIMBING STAIRS OF SUNLIGHT (2013) in the four sacred directions of a spiritual bond that has begun to unite and encourage people from around the world. It draws a circle ever wider to include more and more people without exceptions, without conditions, without any test of their worthiness to be respected and loved. The words in this book are a testament to what we can share in common when we take time to listen, to care, and to love across all boundaries. It is a fear free zone for the human family.

Thank you for stepping into the circle with us. I believe that the more we can share the messages contained in these four books of faith, the more we can bring peace and harmony into the world. And that will make my ancestors proud.

JANUARY

January 1

And so begins again another year of my life with you, another chapter in the book of our shared story, another part of the adventure that has brought us this far. Are you ready? I am. I feel the confidence of experience. I know now that we will be able to handle whatever comes our way. We will do what we always do: make the hard times work, make the good times sing. It will be alright, come what may. We will be together again. Together to explore the distant days and star-strewn nights. Together, O God, in this discovery we call faith.

January 2

Gift your life with small graces, the quiet acts of kindness that you can do, offering patience when you can, the simple sharing of time to listen, the hand of mercy to another, the word of encouragement unexpected. We each have more chances than we know to be a daily blessing. Not a single extravagance of generous behavior, but a list of the good works we can do each day, our spiritual chores, signs of love, beaded together to make a pattern of hope, touching our common life with beauty, turning a colder world warm with the light of understanding.

January 3

In my dream I saw the Spirit open her wings, gathering scores of people beneath her power, and with one swift leap she carried them forward, across the thin line of time from one year to the next. So swiftly did she act that she left the heavy parts of their lives behind, the pain and hurt, the loss and grief, the anger and fear, the illness and sadness: all left standing in the past, unable to follow, while the people were rejoicing in their release. Today is a fresh start. Now is the moment of your freedom. God has given you tomorrow. Feel that new hope rising.

January 5

Restless hearts, restless minds, move like strangers beneath the shadows, searching for an end to their uneasy path, wandering along the edges of safety, waiting alone in crowds that move like dark streams around them. To discover God's purpose, to find meaning in life, to be blessed with a content spirit, these are not easy achievements in an age unsettled and afraid. Be firm in your faith. Wait for the word in confidence. Do not be swept away in currents of cold worry, but know the warmth of a believing family, your friends standing by you, your soul at rest and ready.

January 6

Time to get my vision checked. I need to make an appointment with God to see how my spiritual eyes are working. Am I seeing the world clearly? Am I looking at the people around me with a bright view? Or are there blind spots in my perception of reality? Do I have a loss of clarity, a graying of my vision, a distorted opinion of the distance between me and those for whom I should care? I never take it for granted. I never assume I can see perfectly. I take the time to let the expert check me out, to test my sacred sight and help me look at life without blemish.

January 7

Heal the secret hurts within, those deepest memories we all carry, but rarely even mention, the very private pain that seems to be our inheritance, given to us even in childhood, or acquired over a lifetime, moments when we endured, but never forgot, keeping our vigil over a hidden past, wearing the unseen sadness for years. It is on these most tender places, for both you and I, that I pray God places a gentle hand, drawing out the sorrow, restoring lost innocence, healing us as an act of liberation, a gift of freedom from the secret hurts within.

January 8

Let not the hope of the poor be taken away. Let not the dreams of hard working people be lost. Let not the woman or man searching for work be disappointed. Let not the few keep more than they need while the many are left without enough. Let not the world be divided by those who have and those who are denied. Please hear these prayers, God, and give us the will to live them out. Strengthen our resolve for justice, for fairness in the marketplace, for an honest chance for every person who works for their family. Let us earn so that we can share.

January 9

When I am only a memory, a whisper on the wind, you may still hear my words speaking to you, like an echo of a dream, a lost thought brought back to mind. And the same will be true for you. We will not disappear from this world, though we no longer walk beneath its warm sun, for our presence will still be felt, even across the timeless river that separates our new home from these familiar places. We will always be a blessing to those who call us to mind, a feeling of comfort, a sense of direction, a gift of wisdom. Our life is never done, our work for love only just begun.

January 10

I pray your peace in troubled lands, in places where people fear each day, in cities or villages under threat of danger. I pray your peace into the hearts of those who hate, into the minds of those who live in anger, of those who long for revenge. The hot winds of war sweep over so many lives, dear God, terror and cruelty following in their wake, I do not know what else to do, but stand here making my appeal to heaven. Peace I pray. Peace against all the odds, peace without compromise, peace strong and enduring, peace so children never worry as they go to sleep.

January 12

It is at quiet times like this that I know God cares for you, for me, for all of creation. I cannot reason it out or explain it. I cannot prove it to you and I would not try. I just know that a hand comes to wake me, unseen, unbidden, into these still hours, and as I pray in obedience to that call I feel the presence of a love that transcends description. Here, in this place with me, right now, is enough goodness to touch every beating heart that ever longed for love. God is real. And aware. And very beautiful. I cannot say more, but in saying it, I hope I have awakened you into the quiet with me.

January 13

Low the angels fly, with unseen wings outspread, riding the currents of air that flow like a river between heaven and our earthly home. They drift down to watch over us, to keep us as safe as they can, year after year, through every season of our lives. You may smile and say it isn't so, that what I tell you now is only a wistful remnant of a childhood storybook, but pause before you laugh. Have you never been pulled back from harm? Have you never wondered how and why? It is not someone "up there" watching over you, but someone standing by your shoulder.

January 14

God and I are very busy. We are forever working. I am usually very occupied designing and digging canals, those little moats that separate me from others. I have canals based on my education, my race, my class, my religion, my gender or age, lots of little canals to maintain. Meanwhile, God is building bridges. I will stop to help with that at times, but I still want to have my canals. So we live in Venice. And at the end of the day, we take a gentle cruise through the city on my boat, although God always enjoys inviting others to come along for the ride.

January 15

I have a romantic attachment to SETI, the search for extraterrestrial intelligence, a decades long project that listens on radio telescopes to hear any sounds from alien broadcasts outside our solar system. On August 13, 1977, they heard one. It lasted 72 seconds, but was not repeated, so it can't be official proof. They called it the Wow! signal. I used to want to be a SETI technician. A listener. Then it struck me: I already am. Every day I listen for messages from God, a genuine extraterrestrial intelligence. And I hear those signals over and over. Wow!

January 16

This dark night too shall pass away, this long struggle will come to an end. No matter how difficult any moment in your life may seem, it is always just that, a moment, a season of trouble that rises up like a storm, but in time will spend its energy and drift away on God's returning breeze. Do not be afraid that hardship is forever. Do not despair that you have forgotten how to laugh. The power of love is stronger than sorrow, the healing of hope more certain than any sadness. A holy heart hears your prayers and even now is coming so swiftly to find you.

January 17

Like all religious people I am sometimes bewildered by those who don't believe. I am never upset or angry by their opinion, but just curious about how they can be so certain that nothing exists out there but mechanical principles. And then I think even if they were right, even if they could finally convince me we were alone, I would still go on believing. I would stand alone, a tiny speck of life in a vast uncaring Universe, and with all the strength I had I would lift my voice to sing, sing the human heart, sing joy and love and peace to echo and echo for all time to come.

January 19

I pray that what you have to confront today will be enough for tomorrow too, that you will not have any more needs to face, any more items to add to your list of things to do, but have the time you need to deal with what you have. If this is not a prayer you need right now, then save it for another day, but if you are juggling as fast as you can, then receive this as a blessing. How often we think we can make it, if only life will let us finish one challenge before offering us the next. Let my words balance your load, a helping hand just when you most could use it.

January 20

We hope for things unseen, but I also think we hope for things in plain sight. I hope for my family, for friends that I know are facing difficult times, for the community in which I live, for the corner of this Earth that I call home. My hope is rooted. It is grounded in reality. I hope for what I can touch and feel, what I share in every day, what I see in the eyes of others. Hope is what we have when we have little more. It has to be seen. It has to be tangible. So yes, I do hope long distance, but I also hope up close and personal, hope so near to me I never lose sight of it.

January 21

I have been asked to speak to young adults on the subject of inter-faith cooperation. I can think of few subjects more important. For so many centuries religion has been (and continues to be) a force for dividing humanity. The irony of faith as a weapon should never be lost on us. It has cost every nation and every faith community a great price. But the reverse can be true, the blessing of mutual respect, kindness and cooperation. The issue is not who is right, not if we truly practice what we preach. The issue is: what would God have us do together?

January 22

Love is not constrained by the imagination of time, but continues through eternity, as surely as any force known to physics, constant in presence as possibility, ever able to appear in any feeling mind or heart, gently in innocent nurture, passionately in young desire, weaving life into the cold matter of our physical being, energizing history into becoming, changing the equation of the spirit to be more than ever alone it could have dreamed. The love you share now will last forever. The love you feel was felt a thousand years before. In love you live and will live again.

January 23

Here is to friendships, old and new, that bond our lives to past and future, the swing of the garden gate, that dance across the floor of time, moving from memory to maybe, all in one evening. Last night I sat at dinner with two old friends I had not seen for years. Two new friends sat with us, drawing the circle together. Past and future, familiar faces and newborn visions, talking through the night, laughing through the night, becoming a community one friend at a time. We are what we are because we share what we are with those we know and those we want to know.

January 24

On a cold winter's afternoon, I stood alone beneath the high vaulted ceiling of the chapel at Trinity College, where I had once sat as a student over forty years ago, where I had once returned to be chaplain near twenty years ago, where I had once prayed, once laughed, once lived among so many moving now like shadows, the sound of distant singing, my once and future life, lived here beneath this high vaulted ceiling, living still in the echo of my memory, here on a quiet afternoon's reminder that we are all but a breath away from what once seemed so real.

January 26

I write these meditations as they come to me, not trying to force or control what they say, following my fingers as they type where my heart leads me, letting the whispers of the spirit guide me in all I do. To do this is not a trick, but a simple practice of a deeper lesson. In our spiritual lives we learn to let go, to trust, to follow, giving over our need to control to the direction of a deeper wisdom. Yes, I do my part, I write the words of my own story, but the author is another voice, wiser by far and more loving than I may ever hope to be, though I write for all eternity.

January 27

You are a good person. That may not seem like much of a compliment, but consider what it says about you. It means that you are aligned with the ancient forces that bring goodness into our world, the cause of justice, the expression of compassion, the offer of comfort and mercy to all in need. You are not perfect, but you are a living symbol of hope for others to see and emulate. You strive for virtue, dignity and honor. You walk the path of righteousness, trying your best to be truthful and fair. Yes, I see it in you, and am proud to say it of you: you are a good person.

January 28

I have seen the world ahead, the one peeping at us through the cracks in our own history. I wish I could say it was a perfect world, where all our struggles are ended, but you would know that could not be true, given the nature of our freedom as a human family. But I can say the place looks much better than today, so we must be doing something right. We finally agreed to disagree, letting each other sleep more safely, and turned our hand to fixing the Earth, no longer so badly battered. We have a future after all, a chance to give peace a try and justice a home in who we are.

January 29

One more prayer. I will say one more prayer, even if I feel I have prayed an ocean dry, or have repeated this same thought a thousand times. Silence does not intimidate me but invites me, a chance to share once more the longing of my spirit for an answer. Insistent in faith, not demanding, but ever present, standing there still, even after everyone else has left, praying on into the waiting hours, willing to out-wait even them. One prayer more, for you, for the hungry, for the poor, for the lost, for the found, for what I hope even when hope has given in to sleep.

January 30

I believe one of the things our world needs now, more than ever, is a renewed sense of the transcendent. We have lost our capacity to feel in awe. Therefore, we have lost our humility. We live in an age that imagines we are in control, mesmerized by the latest gadgets of our own creation, assuming all of the answers will soon be within our utilitarian grasp. We make money, not dreams. We look at screens, not the sky. We are diminished by the delusion of greatness. I pray a renewal of breathless wonder back into our lives, a return to speechless love before the holy.

Janury 31

If I had to express how I believe in only a very few words, I would say that it comes down to this: I am to take care of the loving and let God take care of the judging. And I like it that way. I am blessed to be under such a rule. It frees me from fear. It allows me to listen and learn. It gives me the grace to let others be who they are without the need of my correction. It keeps me from narrow mindedness and pinched self-assurance. It opens my heart. My work is compassion, kindness, and healing without exception. I leave the rest to the One who made us all.

FEBRUARY

February 2

I have encountered God in the unexpected and lost God in the familiar. I have been carried on people's shoulders and been thrown beneath the bus. I have discovered the sacred in places of struggle and the humble in places indolent with privilege. I have searched like a miner for meaning and practiced the science of wonder. I have walked empty halls called holy, heard wordless sermons, listened to songs of adoration gone suddenly silent. I am a doubter by trade and a disciple by vocation. Like all seekers, I have a long story to tell, full of the beauty and pain of living.

February 3

However dark the path behind you, that much more light awaits you on the path ahead. Do not stop in despair and imagine that you are defined by what you have suffered. Your faith defines you, your dignity, courage and wisdom. Many of us have gained our love through the struggles we have known. Without those sorrows we would not so quickly see the blessings that surround us nor count them so precious for knowing life without them. So raise your head and let the angels see the truth in your eyes: you are not the child of fear but born to be stronger than death.

February 4

God is in the kitchen, sitting quietly over a cup of coffee. God is on the street corner, waiting for the light to change. God is at the bar, watching the game on tv. God is in the beauty shop, listening to the latest stories. There is no place where we are that God is not. No moment when we cannot turn to find God available. We build our sanctuaries more for ourselves than for our Maker, who calls the whole creation home, and moves with ease among us, as ordinary as sunlight, as close as a whisper, right where you would hope to find the holy, just there beside you.

February 5

Let us be grateful for the small things, the common blessings that grow around us like wild flowers. How easy it is to rush past them. Our minds become so accustomed to worry, we forget what it feels like to simply be present to the goodness that is our inheritance. Watch the children who are our guides, in the playground, at the store, wherever they may be, these young souls are our reminders to draw in the innocence of God, the playful joy that surrounds us, the wonder at being able to be alive. Give thanks for tangible grace, for people who care, for love and for laughter.

February 6

What can I give that will help? I think that is such a simple but important question. Sometimes I am tempted to close my ears to the appeals I hear, thinking myself overwhelmed by the cries of those in need, too poor to give more than what I already offer, indignant that I should be pressed yet again to share what I have. Then I think of the generosity of God, who spared nothing to give to me, to you, to the billion faces upturned in prayer every day, giving and giving, grace upon grace, joyous and abundant, a cup running over in love. What can I give that will help?

February 7

As communities of faith, we walk the high-wire act, the tightrope, of difference. Suspended far above the depths of our own history, across the millennia of our cultural evolution, we step out to keep our balance when it comes to difference. On one side is the diversity that makes us strong. On the other, the fear that makes us fragment. How we conceive of difference determines destiny. In the eyes of God we are a joyful variety of the very same substance. In the end, the long wire of race, religion, gender, class, sexuality and ethnicity will be the test of our future as the people of God.

February 9

If you listen on quiet nights, when only the stars are awake, you can hear the sound of laughter, falling faint but clear through the icy air. It is the voice of our elders, gathered by glowing hearths in heaven on high, telling their stories, sharing their memories, ringing in the peace that surrounds them with a joy that chimes the ageless hours of their lives. They call us to remember that we need never fear these short days, for they are only a faint vision passing, while more life still waits for us, in the lighthearted halls of our other home among the ones we love.

February 10

We are disciples of the God of questions. More than just a rule of answers, the dead-end of spiritual curiosity, our God invites us ever forward, following the endless path of why. Surely no gift in our creation has been greater than the gift of human reason, the ability to think, to wonder, to analyze and understand. The great Mind that gave us this ability certainly did so in the hope that we would use it. Our faith, therefore, is not a law but a lab, a place of inquiry, a process by which we come to learn, and in the learning, love.

February 11

The Spirit seeks the silent soul, the one too shy to speak, who seems lost in the pressing crowd, a small island in the midst of the great sea, a person on the back pew, the quiet girl who rarely speaks, the boy least likely to be noticed, an honest life without adornment. Healing to this gentle heart, strength and comfort ever present, for no human story goes unheard, no life unnoticed by God, whose Spirit moves to choose the one standing alone, to grasp the hand of the last in line, and lift up that soul from silence, beautiful and light, rising in joy to be so free to sing.

February 12

I am often haunted by the thought that somewhere out there is someone who needs help, but I have no way of knowing who they are or where they are or what they need. It may be my spiritual imagination playing tricks on me, but I feel them calling out, silently, into the wideness of the world, casting their hope into a bottle tossed on the restless sea, calling out to you and me. Please join me in a prayer, a lifeline thrown out in love, to anyone out there, whoever they may be, a life rescued, a life restored, a life valued and loved, unknown but not forgotten.

February 13

The candle burns low. I have said all the prayers I can say. I wait in the silence to hear any word returning from the far side of what I know. Outside the wind wraps a cold arm around the moon and the trees wave their empty hands in surrender to the season. We each find our own way to the borders of the sacred. We each learn to listen. There is no religion when we are alone, just the wonder of a longing heart, the intimate wait when all the prayers are done. May you discover what you seek. May you hear an answer on the wind. May love find you before the candle goes out.

February 14

It is time for me to renew my license to practice what I preach. That means I have to take my annual witness test. What do people see when they watch what I do? In politics do they see me express my opinions with civility and respect those who disagree with me? In religion do they observe me as faithful to my beliefs and loving in my attitude toward those who pray differently? In economics do they see me live in simplicity and generous in sharing what I have? In creation do they see me care for the Earth and nurture life with my choices? Time for some honest answers.

February 16

How can I not be merciful to others when God has been so merciful to me? How can I not show compassion since I have received the blessings of compassion so often in my life? How can I not love those who most need love because I have been loved by a holy love when others would never have wanted me? Practicing the spiritual life is not hard. It is simply a matter of copying what we have already learned from God. We are the image in the mirror, moving to mimic what we see, reflecting grace in what we do, returning the kindness we have received.

February 17

Peace to us all. To those of us who believe in God and those of us who don't. To those who think the best expression of their political opinions is anger and to those who find their religion makes them afraid of others. To the people who have it all and still want more. To the ones who pray they have enough to get through the night. To the dreamers and the realists, to the inmates and the seekers, to the night club crowd and the people with a liturgical fetish. To people of every sort and condition, peace, to the fullness of humanity, peace, to us all, each and every one, peace.

February 18

G ood news is coming, flying on the wind, wings out-stretched, racing the rivers of air to find you. The answer to your prayers, longed-for hope, darting past the clouds, out running the shadows, sparkling beneath the sun of your new horizon. Look up and feel that fresh breeze of the Spirit moving around you. Your words have not been lost, your need not forgotten, your dreams have caught the song of life and reached all the way to heaven. Good news is coming. Now is your time, now your moment of completion. Listen, something of wonder comes your way.

February 19

T he love of God rests on me like a shawl placed around the shoulders of an elder fallen asleep by the window. Outside the world moves on through its busy pace, children run through the yard, the dog barks, the neighbors talk about the weather. Every moment of life is filled with the beauty of simple being, every moment holds the possibility of unexpected grace. Kindness spreads like sunshine, mercy comes down like rain. How much of this sacred balance depends on the dreams of God and how much on the dreams of the elder? A little of both I think.

F e b r u a r y   2 0

Please God, give me the time to love as long as I can. Let it not be a love measured out in the small portions of my own need, but given away so freely that it reaches as many other lives as possible. Let it be as gentle as laughter and as strong as courage. Let it touch the ones I would turn to as well as the ones from whom I would turn away. Help me to be an oasis of love for the wandering soul, a rock of love for the soul at risk, a shelter of love for the weary and the innocent. No other request but this, please God, let me love as long and as well as I can.

F e b r u a r y   2 1

I honor my son today for all the lessons he taught me. He showed me things I would never have seen, kept me honest, helped me discover the integrity of spirituality grounded in disciplines that set the spirit free. We learn from the young as well as the elders. Listen to the youth of our time and place, respect them and give them a place at the table. For it is through these young women and men that tradition is more than a museum and faith grows into time to bless and bless again. Without my son I would not be what I may still become. Thank you, Nick.

February 23

If this is a difficult time for you, or for someone you know, let me speak a clear word straight to your heart: there is no trouble stronger than the love of God. There is no illness, no broken relationship, no financial setback, no personal hurt that the love of God cannot heal. Not even death can overcome it. That love is for you. It may come to you as you read these words or it may take time, but it will come to you: the assurance, the comfort, the renewal of a love that will embrace you and hold you and abide with you, until the light returns and departs no more.

February 24

Let us dare to love one another, all of us, no matter how different we may be, no matter how stern the rules that forbid us to appear in public together. Let us climb over the high walls of our own doctrine, sneak past the guards of the caste systems that tell us we are never to speak to those people, and see what it feels like to be out under the open sky. For too long our religious fences and racial fears have kept us hidden, now is the moment for our peaceful insurrection. Let us dare to love, to listen, to learn, to be the friends our common spirit tells us we are and always were.

February 25

O Gracious Light, guide me into the shimmering, into that place where only the purity of holy candles burn, small flickers against the dark, glowing in hope, warming in hope, setting the still air to breathe. The light of God shines gently for each one of us, a beacon through the storm, a companion in the night journey, a sign of welcome in the window at road's end. O Gracious Light, the ancient words sing again, ringing out the blessing of clarity, of vision, of renewal for all who wake to wonder, for all who open their eyes to see bright love standing right before them.

February 26

I invite everyone to join me in living a fear free day. No matter how grave my own situation may seem, no matter how difficult the struggles of the world, I want to live these hours without being afraid. I will believe that my life is in the hands of a loving power that will help me find my way through any hardship. I will believe that peace and goodness will heal the broken world in which we live. I will not despair. I will not surrender to resignation. I will let my fears go, dropping them at my feet, as I rise to feel the lightness of my spirit when all it knows is faith unfettered.

February 27

May God watch over you in the quiet hours, the private moments in your daily life when your thoughts slip sideways into the still spaces of your soul. These are the times when you are most with yourself. They are a place where only you can go, that inner sanctuary of every life, the deep center, where we are who we are when no one else is watching. In good days and bad, we return. In deep thought and peaceful dreaming, we find our inner home, the source and the vision. May God wait on you there, to speak if needed or to sit in silence, the heart of your contemplation.

February 28

I have been studying the life of Gandhi again, watching the old tapes of his work in India, reading his words on non-violence and justice. He never fails to inspire me, even though his legacy remains flawed. Gandhi said that we could not use religion as a mask for discrimination of any kind. He said that once a nation begins to use religion for partisan purposes it ceases to be a democracy. When religion becomes a tool it also becomes a weapon. Therefore, democracy has no caste systems. I honor the Mahatma for his wisdom. Truth is truth in any faith or nation.

MARCH

M a r c h   2

God drive back the dark days of war, place your angels between innocent lives and the tread of advancing tanks, cool the political fires that burn for power and greed, let wisdom prevail and compassion increase. We feel the storms of war in so many places these days, we know the suffering armed conflict brings to elders and to children. Spare us more wars in our time, great God of peace, and shelter your people from death and destruction. Let our prayers rise to you, let justice stand guard over every border, love in every land, that no lives be lost to the hungry heart of hate.

M a r c h   3

When the times in which we live become uncertain, when we begin to doubt our own place in history, then even the words we use seem to melt in their meaning. What is justice? What is truth, or nation, or family, or law? We are not sure. Some claim an answer and call the fearful to stand by their flag. Others drift with no answers into an ethical fog. If we are wise and faithful, let us stand firm against the pull to an extreme and by our own calm assurance that no time is out of God's care, let our words take the shape of hope unafraid, a clear call to every unshaken spirit.

M a r c h   4

Last night I met with a group of Native American scholars with whom I am working on a project of both mind and heart. It was a quiet gathering, a simple sharing of ideas and visions, but the feeling it created within me has lasted well into this new day. Tradition is wisdom collected. Wisdom is experience gathered. Experience is life encountered. We are all scholars of our own story and of other stories we learn through love. When we share what we know, what we value, we spin a force of the Spirit that reaches back to ancient campfires and out to a tomorrow we cannot yet imagine.

M a r c h   5

I like old-fashioned values. Courtesy and kindness, honor and integrity, modesty and civility. I like new-fangled ideas. Pluralism and diversity, equality and individuality, innovation and expression. I am an old-fashioned new-fangle. Life is best along the edges, where we bring our past with us as we step out into a new beginning. Values are our compass, we are meant to use them as we navigate uncharted waters. Change is tradition growing. I do not want to live in a museum any more than I wish to exist in chaos. Wander free, let wisdom find the border.

March 6

I spent the evening listening to a Native elder, a woman who has changed history by her drive and imagination. She laughed and said that her vision was really very simple: don't just talk, do something. There is truth in what she says. How often we find leadership lost in endless spirals of analysis or debate. The willingness to move, to try something, to get off the ground is left at the starting gate, talked into a corner and kept there by the inertia of contingencies. Let us feel the spirit of creation. Let us be hearers and doers, people whose faith is more a verb than a noun.

March 7

If I could not speak, would people still be able to tell that I was a person of faith? If I could not write, would they know how much I believe? Could they tell just by watching me? Could they see the light of kindness in my eyes, the depth of compassion in my touch? Would I truly be an outward and visible sign, even if I had no way to communicate save by my actions? I pray that the answer would be yes. Yes, for you and for me, yes to a life lived so clearly in devotion that no words would be needed to proclaim the simple truth of its love.

March 9

Turn to the wisdom within, seek out what you have learned over years of experience. Be guided by these lessons from life, study them well and remember what you felt and what you feel still, deep in the heart of your memory. We each carry this gift of our own common sense. We have paid the tuition of long nights and hopeful days to learn what we value. We have made discoveries that delighted us and closed some doors we will never again want to open. Look out in prayer to the voice of God to see what to do, but turn to the wisdom within to know how to do it.

March 10

You are here for a reason, a reason that is defined not only by the work you do, but by the life you lead. You are a connecting point for the sacred, a living channel through which streams of grace flow, flow out into the world, into the reality of the people you meet, into the world you help to create simply by your presence. You are a signal, a messenger who lives the message, who embodies the meaning of the holy in every choice you make. You are a healer, a source of nurture and wholeness, here for a reason, a reason that restores the bridge of hope.

March 11

I understand why we say that we carry guilt. It is because that emotion seems to have such weight. It is a burden that each of us bears. For some of us it is a quiet acceptance of a memory we carry as our due, but for others the feeling can be crushing. There is no quick fix to guilt. It is a process of reconciliation, restoration, forgiveness and healing that takes time and special pastoral care. But the effort is worth the return for we are not expected by God to walk this life weighted by endless guilt. Let us pray we each find our inner peace and step more lightly toward tomorrow.

March 12

We are the architects of our own lives. God is a carpenter who helps us construct what we design. We have the freedom to imagine dwelling places far too grand and when the plan begins to fall apart turn to the wisdom of experience to save the house from falling. We can resign ourselves to something far too cramped for our spirit's shelter only to delight in how the builder has opened up new spaces for us. In the end, we are allowed to be ourselves, to fashion who we are, but what remains most lasting in life is the craft of the One who worked beside us.

M a r c h   1 3

It will be like this: when we close our eyes one last time, and draw in the breath that unlocks us from this life, then the cage of time will be open to us, setting us free from the measure of minutes, releasing us into the limitless sky, to soar above the waters like sea birds, darting over the waves in sparkling light, feeling the rush of new life like morning air, spiraling out and up and over, delighting in the weightless elegance of love, our souls dancing above the shores of space, rising up into sunlight, like sea birds, flying, flying on outspread wings of joy.

M a r c h   1 4

Be healed of what harms you. Be whole and free and restored to the fullness of your life. Be strong in your spirit. Be clear in your mind. Be unafraid and confident of what is to come. Be renewed in your faith. Be renewed in your hope. Be renewed in your love. Let all of these blessings surround you. Let them enfold you. Claim them and build your future on them. They are your birthright. They are the truth beneath your struggles. They are the enduring grace that forever seeks to find you. Take this gift of blessing. It is for you. It is why you awoke this day. It is your new life.

March 16

If I could reach around the world, and hold every life in peril safe from harm, I would not hesitate to see who I might embrace, but gather them up without a second thought. Let me remember that image in my daily life. Let me speak well of people of every place, every faith, every culture and condition. Let me make no distinctions in my kindness, but extend respect to all. For by so doing I may be that lifeline of blessing to someone I do not know, to someone as in need of compassion as I am. God plays no favorites nor will I, but reach out in love as far as love can go.

March 17

Last night I prayed for an elder who is going to have surgery. His daughter and wife were there. We talked as we sat in their living room, talked like the rural Oklahomans we are, talked in our own accent, talked of the red earth, open skies, free spaces, grassland fields, where you go down to water the horses. It reminded me why I am home, home to the far horizon country, to where prayers are made of clouds and wind. I prayed for him in that voice, calling the Spirit from the Oklahoma night, to this family of my same soil. Wherever you are from: there God is.

M a r c h   1 8

I have been watching two young lives unfold, doing my best to keep up, the old man following along behind, marveling at how they move so gracefully through their days, effortless in love, confident in the future they make with a smile, so much energy pouring out in laughter, flying through the sunlight with time to spare, love a force that cannot be stopped, youth eternal in the touch and shared feeling. Surely God is not always the ancient of days, but the young at heart and spirit, the just starting, the new creating, the always youthful God of joyful discovery.

M a r c h   1 9

I pray through the night on tribal lands, here in the place where my ancestors first arrived on the Trail of Tears, the old land, sanctified by their struggle, made holy by their survival. Deep in the night I hear the sound of a passing train, its mournful call carrying the lament of history over the sleeping fields, calling me to follow the tracks of history to know the truth of my own tribe of origin. We are all citizens of our shared past, shaped through stories once lived, educated by memory, blessed by those who went before, following them into the still night of trains and dreams.

M a r c h   2 0

You are of more value than can be measured on the scale of material design. In the eyes of God, you are beloved, held as dear to heart as any child ever born to any parent whose longing to love had reached the edge of forever. You are more than simply important, you are needed, you are a cornerstone to someone's dream, an answer to prayer for those you touch each day. You are light in the evening shadows, a beautiful reminder that we are each born to bless, a living song that makes even the sad soul smile and the old memory rejoice. You are hope. You are healing. You are a gift. Believe in who you are and treat your life with care.

M a r c h   2 1

For all the young parents, walking their new babies to sleep through the early morning hours, for all the job hunters, searching for the work they need, for all the late night care givers, keeping watch under the eye of the moon, for all the families under stress, trying hard to make ends meet this month, for all the elders, sitting quietly with their thoughts, for all the students, climbing the steep hills of learning, for all the people of faith, whatever their faith may be, for all the dreamers, still seeing visions of beauty, for all the children, living in every land: blessing, God's perfect peace.

M a r c h   2 3

I am praying where I am, you are praying where you are, around us millions are praying in their own places and their own times. I am praying in my language, you in yours, and together with so many others our sacred words rise to heaven in a thousand dialects of the human voice. I am dreaming my holy dreams, you are dreaming, the whole world is dreaming, spinning out our hope like ribbons caught on the morning air. God is watching over me, God is watching over you, God is watching over every soul that lives beneath the stars we share.

M a r c h   2 4

L et us renew our vows of service, offering what we have to the work of God, keeping our sacred contract of faith, being active in the cause of what is good and right and compassionate. Let us give our minds to truth, our hearts to love, our hands to justice. If we can hold these three vows before us, making them our commitment each day until they are the second nature of our vocation, then we can search for truth, reach out in love, and build a more just community. May God hear our intention and bless us each into the keeping of it through the sealing of the Spirit.

March 25

Like most people, when I pray, I imagine my words and thoughts to be ascending, going up to God who is somewhere above me. But prayer is as horizontal as it is vertical, not only because the presence of God is everywhere around us, but also because our prayers for one another flow out to surround us with a sacred energy, an energy of healing and compassion. Prayers rise, and descend, and encircle. They are in all places at all times, a living hope constant in our lives, a force of life that knows no barrier nor boundary, but touches even the most distant need.

March 26

Each year when tax season rolls around I start thinking of all the families who struggle to have enough to keep them going. My heart embraces the hard working women and men who do all they can to make it to the end of the month. I consider the elders living on fixed incomes and the children wishing they could have something special that costs just too much for their folks to afford. Money is not the answer, but it is a constant question. Give help to those in need, O God, with blessings of income that bring them the resources they need the most.

March 27

What message would I leave behind for others to find? What memory or expression of me, left at a favorite spot, beneath a glade of trees where I once lingered, or beside the open sea where I stood watching distant sails trace their finger across the horizon? What words could I use to say what I felt, who I was, something to pass to a stranger, perhaps years and years from now, that would make them not a stranger in the instant of human recognition, a discovery of our shared life in this single space? I would leave this behind for them to see: I knew peace in this place.

March 28

Drift away now, out onto calmer waters, where the breeze takes you, without effort, without direction, following only the current of deeper thought, toward the answers you need, the support of true friends, the love for which you have waited. The spiritual life is not a struggle. Even when it confronts the greatest trials of our time, the hardest transitions of our lives, it is not a power that requires the exercise of force. It is in letting go that we take hold. It is in trust that confidence arises. Let God guide you and you will never fear the storm.

March 30

I am a fan of Dr. Who. He is a time traveler who zips through the universe having adventures. His time machine is the Tardis, a blue box just slightly larger than a phone booth. But when you step inside, it is huge. I think we are like that. Bigger inside than we seem outside. In mind, heart and spirit, we always have more room to encompass reality. Just when we think we are finished, along comes a new idea, a new person, a new wonder to bring within ourselves and embrace. And that is why, like Dr. Who, we have a whole universe to explore. The adventure continues.

March 31

L ost. Yes, I have felt lost in my life, haven't you? Confused, overwhelmed, not sure which way to turn. Maybe now for old veterans of the Spirit like you and me it is not so likely, but for younger souls than ours it is always a real possibility. So join me in sharing your story. Let them know that when and if they ever feel lost they need not be afraid. Help will be coming swiftly, if only they will call on the Spirit to come to find them, lift them up, and hold them safe. That will work. You and I can testify to that fact, because it worked for us, once, long ago, when we were lost.

APRIL

April 1

It is in the quiet hours, the still spaces between demand and need, that we can find God patiently waiting, like an elder reading a book, dozing gently the dreams that make our world, listening for the sound of rain, keeping watch over the gentle hearts that pray in whispers, remembering all the good times that give memory its warmth, the God of stories told to children, of late night truth telling, of comfort and of courage, yes that God, the forever companion, wisdom beneath eyes that see to the very beginning, God of the quiet hours, of love and of meaning.

April 2

Here is a prayer for healing. Please receive it if you are waiting for lab results. Please receive it if you are undergoing treatment. Please receive it if you have a chronic illness. Please receive it if you are facing surgery. Please receive it if you are working a program of rehab. Whatever struggle or need you may have, please receive the prayer that comes from one frail life to another, receive the blessing that flows from one brave spirit to another, receive the love that reaches out from stranger and friend alike. Most of all, receive the healing of God. Be lifted up in the arms of holy care, be whole in every part, every part, of your mind and body.

April 3

There is a light that shines for each one of us, no matter how dark the world around us. It is a light we can see with eyes of our soul, a single glow on the distant horizon, never fading, never changing, constant in its bright presence. That light is the love that never wavers. It is a sign that God is there, believing in us, watching over us, standing guard on the borders of our heart. There is no person who is not beloved of God. There is no one who is without the light, even if they choose not to look at it. May that light touch you with hope today and guide you on the path to peace as you travel toward its source.

April 4

Over the years I have sat in many airports, watching the crowds pass by, a steady stream of faces, some happy, some anxious, people alone or in families, with friends or just moving among strangers. Each time I see this parade of who we are I am reminded of our diversity and of our vulnerability. For all of our numbers, in such a vast array of shapes and sizes, colors and coverings, we are only a river of separate lives, small hopes embodied, tender feelings behind the busy mask, a walking memory of all that we have seen and done, wanting to get somewhere, wanting to arrive. May each one of us travel in safety as we pass by.

A p r i 6

L ast night I had a chance to talk over dinner with a very
wise woman, Krista Tippett, whose radio program on
NPR, "On Being", is one of the most important conversations
on religion taking place in America today. One of the issues
she and I share is the question of civility: how can we learn
to talk with one another about our disagreements in a
courteous, compassionate and constructive way? Too often
people only shout their opinions in the public forum. How
do we speak in a way that creates community? I was proud
to say that this community is one small answer. Thank you
all for making it so. You are the hope we need.

A p r i 7

I have the feeling that you are about to receive a touch of
inspiration. Don't ask me why, it's just another holy
hunch. But the feeling is there, like the scent of rain on the
wind, a small thought hiding behind the daily chores,
peeping out to tease me into realizing that the Spirit is at
work around me, a movement of sacred energy starting to
build on the horizon of prayer. Open your mind. Calm your
mind. Let the pathways to your soul be clear, let go of the
same old same old, because I have this feeling that you will
be receiving a touch of divine wing as it passes by you one
day soon on its way to wonder.

A p r i l   8

In how many ways can I be kind? How can I express my affection or my respect? What can I do to show compassion or extend encouragement to others? The terrain of possibilities for me to practice what I preach is without limit or boundary. The options are beyond number. The key is not to wait until I stumble upon such an opportunity, but to be intentional about finding or making these moments happen. Virtue is a pattern in life, not a discovery. We become more conscious of how to lead a life of service to others by keeping that goal before us each day. Over time we need fewer reminders, but act by our sacred instinct of love.

A p r i l   9

I will be there in the in-between times, says the God of patience, when the hours grow long and the waiting is hard. I will stand beside you, says the God of comfort, when you feel even the weight of thin air about you. I will lay my hand on yours, says the God of healing, and let my life flow into you until you are whole again. I will dance across the floor, says the God of joy, to make you smile in celebration. I will answer your questions, says the God of wisdom, when you burn the midnight oil of knowing. I will meet you at the station, says the God of all eternity, when you cross over the long bridge to find me there on the other side.

A p r i l   1 0

Anun, a priest and a rabbi walked into a bar and the rest is humor history. I wonder if one of these stories is God's favorite joke. There must be one, one punch line that makes the halls of heaven ring with holy laughter. I cannot imagine any home of the Most High that does not sparkle with the good cheer of those who fill its mansions. The first laugh of an infant life must surely be the sound to turn God's head to search for the source, the sheer happiness of innocent hearts must be the reflection of every divine purpose. Let our worship be our joy, our mirth the measure of our praise, and let those thirsty three keep walking in forever.

A p r i l   1 1

Now the peaceful hour begins, this small slice of time between midnight and tomorrow, when all the world is hushed, and only the angels on healing errands fly the empty skies. I sit beside the candlelight and listen for that familiar whisper, the voice just beyond the light, the words that float on thin currents of incense, as if they had been there forever. Wholeness in mind, in body and in spirit. That is the gift the writing carries, out among the angels, out into the sleeping world, scattered beneath the patient moon, for all those who will find it. Open what I mean and let the peace of God enter in, in your mind, your body and your spirit.

A p r i l   1 3

Where do you see God entering into your life? I ask myself that every Palm Sunday. It is a question that never grows old. And at times it is easy to answer. There have been seasons when the arrival of the holy was clear to see, an answer to prayer, a celebration, a time of healing and renewal. But in other years the path taken by the divine was obscure. I watched, I waited, but there was no obvious presence I could claim to be the coming of God into my reality. Palm Sunday is not a predictable ritual, but a symbol for a mystery. God enters in, arrives, but not by our time table. You have to stay alert to know which direction to turn.

A p r i l   1 4

Come let us walk, all of us together, the path of days before us, united in our diversity, free in our spirits, confident in the justice of love, finding peace in every step. We are, even if we do not know it, a movement, a witness, a presence of hope in the world around us, for every time that people set aside their differences and disagreements, and stand up to be a community not a herd, the saints on high rejoice, the poor look up and rejoice, the lands burnt dry with war flow again with springs of life, and the elders watch the horizon for the day they always dreamed. Come let us walk, all of us together, until our cause is won.

April 15

I have spent many a long night beside the hospital bed, praying with family members, walking the halls, waiting, wanting to know what the doctor will say. Each of these experiences has taught me something about what it means to be human. It has shown quite clearly that we are fragile beings. We are truly made of clay, vulnerable to the pressure of time and illness. But it has also shown me that we are strong beyond measure, resilient in love, enduring in hope, constant in faith, with compassion that can never be exhausted. I am in awe of who we are: lives of clay that last through eternity, strongest when we are weak.

April 16

I keep my watch through the night, working the long hours of prayer, sending out signals of hope to those who will receive them, asking for healing for those in need, weaving together relationships unseen with an appeal to love, willing with all my heart the peace for troubled lands near and far. I am the night clerk at the front desk of faith, on call for the Spirit that never sleeps, maintaining a vigil that began a thousand years ago, a tradition of grace passed down from heart to heart, against all the odds, believing because I was born to believe, giving what I can, a small light kept on, just in case you need a last minute blessing.

April 17

You will find your way, even if the path before you seems hidden. You will know the right way to go. There is a guide to help you, a wise counselor in whom you can trust. One of the great gifts of God is this offer of help when we need it most, when we stand uncertain, unsure of what to do. Like lost children we can become confused and frightened. But it is exactly in those moments that the wisdom of God stands by us, leading us to better choices, showing us how our lives can come round right. The Spirit is a compass to our souls, a chart to navigate by when the light grows dim. You will find your way. Never fear. Just ask for directions.

April 18

The faith within you is a story, a story with no beginning and no ending, a story that tells who you are, where you have been, what you have seen and experienced. It is the life story that emerges from your own wisdom and your own joy, your own pain and struggle. It is as intimate as your deepest secret and as open to the world as your greatest gift. Each year that passes adds new chapters, new characters, a twist to the plot you may never have expected, but always your narrative, the chronicle of how you are passing through this brief moment as though it were a novel, read and loved, a book made of shadows and love.

A p r i l   2 0

Bright is the day that dawns with new life, casting death's grim shadow from the garden. Bright is the future for even the most humble soul, rising up in the arms of angels. Bright is the promise to all the Earth, sharing peace among the children of light. Let every voice sing this shining song, for we have been set free, we have been ransomed from our own history, given a chance to live again, to hope again, and to see the healing of God spread like sunlight into the rooms of time. It does not matter how you pray, this day is for you, it is the bright day, the birth day, the day when nothing will ever be the same, save the love that rolls back the stone.

A p r i l   2 1

If I proclaimed a renewal of hope for this sad old world of ours, would you believe me? Would you believe it possible? I would not be dismayed to discover that you had your doubts. The evidence is so clearly against me. So much has been going wrong for so long. But at the risk of seeming foolish I will stand to claim a renaissance, a rebirth of our common spirit. I will announce our goodness as inevitable and our wisdom as enduring. I will not bend my neck beneath the false proof of greed, but claim the coming of our best virtues. We are not done yet in hope unless we choose to deny that hope and by so doing deny ourselves.

April 22

Blessings to you and your house, blessings in abundance. I pray the gates of heaven will be open to you, pouring out grace like sunshine, filling your life with what you need most. I pray for an extravagance of healing, a cup overflowing, a joy so pure it makes you feel you are floating, lifted up, held up, brought to the high place of safety where you can see nothing to the horizon but promise and peace. Some times are just right for the outpouring of the Spirit: let this be one of those times for you. Blessings to you and your house, blessings overdue but returned tenfold, blessings in abundance, in the day of your awakening.

April 23

Up from the dark and fertile soil the angel rose, out of the deep ocean waters, down from the rolling clouds of sweet scented rain, through the mist shrouded mountain forests and over the sleeping plain, the angels of the Earth came from all four sacred directions, bringing with them the totems of all God's creatures, the family of life, gathered to receive the hand of their creator as blessing and benediction. I saw all of this and stood in awe at the majesty of the life we share on this bright blue ball, turning ever so silently in splendor. We are stewards. We are caretakers. We are breath embodied, the kin of all that is and ever was.

A p r i l   2 4

How are your negotiations with God going? Mine are getting a lot more interesting. In the early days of my faith I assumed I was only to stand in a state of perpetual awe before the great throne of God. It would never have occurred to me to raise my voice with a question, a doubt, or complaint. Then over time, as I came to understand that we are called to use our intellect, to speak up for what we believe, to search for meaning not wait passively for it to drop on us from a clear sky, I began to do what the old prophets did: talk to my Maker. Express myself. Be real with God. It is getting a lot more lively now for us. How is it going for you?

A p r i l   2 5

Let my amen be a smile. No matter what I may pray, however serious or solemn, however many names and needs I may lift up, let my final thought, my last sacred gesture, be a quiet smile. It is my way of saying that I have the assurance of God that my prayers have been heard. It says that I am confident of the good my prayers will do. It reminds me that I am at peace as my devotions end because my life and the lives of all those for whom I pray is in the hands of God. So I invite you to join me in letting your amen be a gentle smile, a sign of faith, a blessing of hope unspoken and serene. I smile as I write this. May God smile back.

April 27

I am humbled by the gift of knowing you. How small a thing it is that we gather here for such a short time, and yet how important to us both. We are reminders to one another, reminders that there is something gracious in life, something sincere and honest. Even by our presence in this brief encounter of shared faith we let one another know that belief in goodness and mercy has not become absent from our lives, but rather that it is growing, passing between us and between all of the others we meet here, spreading out through our lives, warming the cold world with love. I am so humbled by the gift you are, to me, and to so many more.

April 28

We will cross that bridge one day, that ancient bridge that spans the dark waters of time. We will find our way to it without even a second thought, walking quietly the path as if we had walked it so often we could do it by memory alone. A distant light, a welcoming light, will seem so familiar, like coming home from a long journey, finding everything just as it should be, safe and secure, back to the place our heart could never leave. There is no dying if there is no death, there is no ending if there is no end, only a passing, a walk across a bridge, a return to a home we never left, a welcome from a face so familiar, and yet, so wondrous.

April 29

I think it is time for a family photo. I am sure from just the right spot in heaven God could get us all in, if we will just squeeze in at the corners. We will need to gather our folks from every continent and nation. We will have to make sure none of the kids are wandering around and get them all to sit down front. We will stand shoulder to shoulder, turning just a little sideways to get everyone in the picture. We will be of all shapes and colors and conditions, God's great family, about to get our picture made so the angels can see what we look like here in 2014. All we need is to call everyone together, and then, on the count of three, say a global "Cheese!"

April 30

What act of grace will you perform today? What blessing will you embody? We are all, each in our own way, agents of God's grace. Every day we are given an opportunity to live out that calling, to be a source of mercy or healing or hope for another human being, perhaps even for many people, or even for the Earth we share with every living creature. Our acts, great and small, matter. They are the endless string of grace that encircles our world like a necklace of light. The choices we make, the things we do, turn the wheel of blessing, bringing goodness into being, kindness into life. What act of grace will you perform today?

M A Y

M a y   1

The sacred books tell us that we are fashioned in the image of God, but what does that mean? There are many answers, but here is one to consider. Many years ago one of my favorite Christian authors, C.S. Lewis, wrote an essay entitled Image and Imagination. I like that connection. I believe that one of the most important things we share with God is the ability to imagine. We are not created to be pious judges of other people's behavior, the chosen few destined for eternity, or the keepers of religions that have become museums. We are created to be spiritual dreamers. To imagine. To wonder. What we share with God is not perfection, but poetry.

M a y   2

Tonight I attended an honoring ceremony for five tribal elders who have served their community with integrity and devotion. Their stories reminded me that community does not just happen. It is not created by laws or legislation. It does not depend on social conformity or political agreement. Community grows when everyday people reach out across all differences to help others. Just that: to help. And from that motivation to help emerges the compassion, vision and hope that transforms strangers into friends. The elders I applauded tonight are a mirror held up to us all. They reflect what is best about us when we care enough to try.

M a y   4

Many years ago I worked at the national offices of my denomination in NYC. Each day into work I passed a few words cut into the stone by the entrance. The words said, "in whose service is perfect freedom". Those words are true. In God there is freedom, a liberation from all that would hold us down or hold us back. Freedom from fear, from arrogance, from isolation. God frees our spirits to be just who we are. God unlocks the prison doors of addiction, bigotry and greed. We are allowed to make our own choices, our own discoveries, our own mistakes. Serving God is the open sky where the soul takes wing, where the heart knows no horizon.

Life is not always easy. Even in the best of times we have our daily cares. And in some seasons of our journey we may wonder if we will be able to take another step. Therefore I want to offer deep prayers of support for those who face struggles. Do not think that you are alone in carrying your burden. You are not forgotten. There are many of us who have known the hardships life can bring and we stand by you in this time of your need. Let us help lift that weight with our understanding and our faith in you. May God's mercy come quickly to renew you in every way, and may you find the peace you hope for in the joy you deserve.

M a y   6

Do not doubt your vision. Do not let it grow dim because you are distracted by so many other cares. Remember it, return to it, and let it enlighten your path once more, showing you why your life is so much a part of the plan of love. You have been given a glimpse into your own future, an echo of the calling that made you choose to walk the path you are on. None of this was by accident. You were singled out for a reason, needed for a purpose. Do not doubt that, but embrace it. Let the vision within you shine brightly now, for soon your gift will be needed as never before. Look, already its light fills your eyes. You believe and so you see.

I have no words tonight, only silence, the silence of an old spirit, sitting quietly in a still night, watching soundless clouds pass beneath the moon. When I was young I read the words of a psalm: for God alone my soul in silence waits. And so it has been, and continues to be, the waiting, the patient waiting, wherever the time or place that draws me into longing. We each wait for God in our own way, sitting in silent memory, praying with sighs too deep for words, longing for that return we know so well. We wait because we believe, watching the horizon of hope for the first sight of faith. We need no words to say what our heart already knows.

M a y 8

There is plenty of room at this table, please pull up a chair and join us, everyone is welcome. There are no strangers in the house of God, only family, only friends, only people like you and me, who believe or doubt, laugh or cry, are found or lost, people who have walked in through any door, through any story, to find themselves in this place, amazed that love invites the unloved, that faith comes in all shapes and sizes, that hope is deeper than dogma. Come rest here. Be at peace. Listen to the sound of countless voices, speaking a thousand languages. This is your home because it has no walls, your shelter because it stands wide open.

M a y 9

Like a beam of sunlight the energy of the Spirit can come to you, warm you and renew you, enlighten your mind with brighter visions for your future, bring you to life, lift you out of the shadows and give you strength to take the next step. Turn to face the sun. Do not look down into the same swirl of dark water that has captured your imagination for too long, but look up to see possibilities grow around you like a field of flowers. Even if your movement is limited, your mind can fly to any corner of reality. You are free, like sunlight, set free by the gift of the Spirit, touched by the mind that first dreamed when all the world still slept, made of grace and wonder.

M a y   1 1

While many affirmations are being offered to women with children, I would like to expand that celebration to speak of how all women, of all ages and all conditions, are mothers to many things in our lives. Women throughout history have been mothers of great invention, creating communities, discovering solutions, healing what harms us, defending the poor, teaching deep wisdom, opening up the vision of what a society can be when it is conceived in justice and mercy. May God bless all these mothers, the ancient heritage of women in every culture and faith, whose leadership and imagination have given birth to a lasting legacy of love.

M a y   1 2

We are so alike, all of us, who carry our quiet burdens, holding our memories like children, afraid to let them go. We become accustomed to the idea of silent struggles. They mark the boundaries of our hope. So we are brave beneath our smiles, never wanting to complain, but waiting to be relieved, even if only for a while. Let that moment come to you now. Hand your hidden heart to God. Share your memories with the Spirit. Be silent no more, but speak the truth of your life in prayer and claim the blessing of renewal. I will ask the same for you, certain that God will hear us, for we are so alike, all of us, who trust a better tomorrow.

M a y   1 3

Joyful banners unfurled, catching the morning breeze beneath an amber sun, leading the tribes of humankind, to walk together the last journey to justice. In time we will see the arc of history turn toward the good; in time we will banish the last of fear. Our long night of struggle will disappear when we feed the hungry, give shelter to the refugee, free the captives, and discover more in common than any difference will ever again deny. The future is not beyond us, but at our feet, waiting in the soil to be brought to life, watered by our shared faith, tended by our courage, the day of liberation like a garden, the song of peace proclaimed by every voice.

M a y   1 4

For each of us there is someone, perhaps one person, a couple, a family, which we hold very close in our prayers. That person, a spouse, a child, a life close to our own, is the focus of a spiritual concern that is beyond words. We long for them to have an answer, to find healing, to be safe. I do not know who this person or persons is for you. I do not know what need there may be that is so near to your heart. But I do know that the authority of God can work miracles in their lives. It is to this desire that I bend my prayers to join you. I put my shoulder of faith against the mountain and pray with the power of love that it be moved.

May 15

In this digital age we are running as fast as we can, trying hard to keep up with the race we have made for ourselves, wanting instant answers to timeless questions, needing ever quicker solutions to ever bigger problems, pushing buttons to type out meaning, upgrading our reality, downloading our understanding, networking with nameless people on distant screens, hurrying to hear the next sound byte, becoming our own software, life as an app, looking into phones to see the other side of the universe. When you get tired, put it down, come over here, sit beside me, watch the clouds, and remember who you are, in no hurry at all.

May 16

I have lived my share of time in the valleys, far down in the dark forest where the sunlight rarely strays, seeing ahead only by short distances, hoping that the path before me will not disappear before I find my way home. In those days what kept me going was faith that one day I would stand again on a higher place, where I could feel the freshness of the air, and see for miles to a bright day breaking over the mountains. If you are in the valley, do not doubt that God will lead you to what you may now only dream. If you stand on the heights, do not forget the grace that brought you there. May God be honored in shadow or in sunlight.

M a y   1 8

I have been having computer problems. It has also reminded me how important it is in spiritual life to stay connected. Spiritual life is not a solo flight across an empty sea. It is a journey of friends. It is a community on the move: elders and youth, men and women, seekers and sages. We learn from one another. We grow together. We find God in our shared experience. The loss of that connection has taught me a valuable lesson. There is no technology to get to heaven, there is only the sound of a quiet voice, the look in familiar eyes, the touch of a gentle hand. You are my gateway to tomorrow. You are the light moving beside me through the night journey to dawn.

M a y   1 9

An old cigar box filled with bottle caps, reds and grays, purple and green, yellow and white, not twist caps like today, old school caps popped off the bottle with a church key, or gathered by little hands from the pop machine at the corner store, when Elvis was new and the summer days lasted forever, a cigar box of jewels, pirate treasure, and dreams of a childhood long past. What you remember from childhood is a code for your Spirit walk. It tells you where you started and what path you took. It whispers about the pure heart of innocence, the early days, when treasures were kept in cigar boxes, and life was still lived as play.

M a y   2 0

Your time starts now. Not tomorrow. Not next week or next month or next year. Not when you are ready. Not when you have enough resources built up, not when you have the plan all arranged, not when you have all the problems solved. It starts now. Because now is the timeless moment of your whole life. Now is the beginning of salvation, of wisdom, of hope, of creativity. God is now. The Spirit is now. You are made of now and to now you will one day return. This is why you were made: to make something out of now, to enjoy now, to live, to live not later, not then, not some day, but to live, fully, completely, freely, now, right now.

M a y   2 1

Here is a seeker's prayer, offered for all who are searching for the Spirit, not inside the walls of faith, but outside, in the open sky of questions, among the uncertain souls who bear the scars of conformity, in the company of mystics and dreamers, religious nomads wandering the far corners of ritual, looking for a truth worth believing, believing goodness is out there, undefined but no less sacred, beneath the moonlight, among the whispers of innocent hearts, a holy hope carried like a gift, brought to the place where God promised to meet us. May all seekers be blessed. May they discover what they seek. May they be heralds of light.

M a y   2 2

I believe there is a spiritual energy that flows through the world. I believe the source of that energy is the Spirit of God, the awareness of human need connected to the compassion of divine intention. I have seen this energy touch people in many ways. I have seen it heal the sick, comfort those in grief, strengthen people who are facing struggles. I know that this energy is not under our control, but I do believe we can ask for it to come into our lives and even direct it toward the good purpose for which we are praying. If you share this belief with me, please join me in calling this gentle power into the life of every person who reads these words. May all be blessed.

M a y   2 3

Light the flame of your imagination. Do not be confined to the narrow vision of cautious minds, but fling wide the doors of your own curiosity. Trust your creative spirit, let it out of the sheltered confines of polite spirituality, allow it to run free into the distant fields of wonder. You were born to be a thinker, a maker, a dreamer, a fashioner of what has never been seen before. You have had this talent since childhood and you know it. You grew up living both here and in places far beyond, places where the very light is different, where music unknown calls the vagabond soul to wander. Take the risk. Be yourself. And watch the stars start to move.

May 25

Look at what you have done. You may not want to hear it, thinking modesty a virtue, or perhaps you are truly not aware of all that you have achieved, but please indulge me this moment of honesty. Look at what you have done: you have worked hard to follow the spiritual path set before you, you have faced the struggles of life, you have cared for others and given all that you can, you have listened and learned, shared in times both sad and joyous, you have used your talent, spoken your mind, carried your burdens, and done all this with quiet courage, the dignity of a free spirit and a generous heart. Look at what you have done and be blessed.

May 26

We remember you. Through all the years and all the changes. Through the memories that make us laugh and the memories that make us cry. We remember you. You are still a part of us and always will be. You are woven into us, knitted into us, wrapped into our hearts like a warm shawl, held tightly in the arms of our love, brought near when the nights grow cold. You live in us. You made that life possible. You sacrificed so that it might be. You walked out before us, sheltered us with your courage, stood guard against our fear, and brought us to this place where our children still play. We will not forget. We will remember you. Always.

M a y   2 7

Sometimes at the midnight hour, just when the sleepy clock on my wall turns its tired face to tomorrow, I think I hear the distant sound of laughter. It is not a loud or insistent sound, but a quiet echo, as if I were in a large house and somewhere in a far room people were enjoying some happy story. I believe when this happens that I am blessed to catch a hint of heaven, allowed only for a second to listen to those who have gone before, just on the other side of the wall of time. Then peace settles back down in my room, the old clock ticks on through the night, and the moon shepherds the stars, as I walk past eternity on my way to bed.

M a y   2 8

I carry the wounded souls of a thousand sorrows in my arms, holding close the pain of as many as I can, to stand before that shrouded altar of hope, waiting patiently to ask for mercy and for justice. It is not an easy thing to believe. There is so much evidence to the contrary. The broken lives of fragile people, people made of glass, of bone and whispered prayers. It takes courage to claim their healing, to expect miracles, to cry out for compassion in the middle of the night. But I am not alone in my intercession, ceaseless for the silent ones, for I know you are there too, caring for all you can. I see you praying, believing, living, so death will never be alone.

M a y   2 9

If you are in need of a smile, I have some extras I am gladly giving away. It seems to me that we have entirely too many frowns going around these days, furrowed brows, pinched eyes, woeful looks. Maybe somewhere along the way we forgot that religion is supposed to make us happy. So please join me in a little holy laughter. It will be good for the soul. And it might bring a little peace into our world. After all, it is hard to be angry when you are smiling. So Muslims and Jews, Buddhists and Christians, Hindus and Taoists, seekers and sought: let's give it a smile and see what happens. If we keep it up, maybe the agnostics will join us. Just sayin'.

M a y   3 0

Open the gates of your love, O God, and let your blessings flow out like water, let them run quickly like streams in the desert, making new paths of hope in old soil, nourishing young lives, overflowing into the places of illness or despair, spreading out to bring joy to whole communities, mingling like rivers to carry weary travelers home, until they come to rest in that gentle sea, that limitless horizon of your mercy. Your people have waited for a very long time, dear God, through many long nights of hurting, through many long days of worry, they have been patient through it all, trusting in your grace and justice. Open the gates of your love.

JUNE

June 1

I am in a very quiet place, far from the rush of ordinary life, embraced by an ancient forest where my ancestors once walked beneath the light of day. I have been listening to the old stories, the memories of my people, spoken in the old language, the sounds of an ancient spirit. I am learning. I am listening. I am growing in wisdom and compassion. We all have a place we can go where we can be young again. We have teachers who can share their vision with us. We have a community that speaks our language. Your past is the doorway into your future. Your tradition is the memory that shapes the dreams you have not yet seen.

June 2

I hope to get home today. I have been on the road and now I will be driving on country roads and highways, through small towns and cities, heading back to my home. And with each mile I travel, I will be thinking how this journey is the universal experience of every human being who has ever lived. We have all been on the road. We are all wanting to get home. We have the feeling that there is some place, located in the geography of our love, where we belong. We have the longing to return. We have the experience of journey. We trust that we will complete the trip safely. I am on the road today, and each of you travels with me, on our way home.

June 3

Listen to the voice within, the one you know so well. You have heard it forming its message in your mind, like a whisper in your ear, words that you recognize as being part of your own spirit, but from some source you cannot claim or control. God offers us insight and understanding, truth and clarity, comfort and courage, if only we choose to hear it, not as the drama of a finger writing on the wall for all to see, but as quiet wisdom that rests like a hand on the shoulder. Be still, be alert, be open to what you may be receiving. It is meant just for you: an answer to your question, a direction for your faith, a healing for your heart.

June 4

I have danced with life as though it were my partner, swinging circles around the floor, without a care in the world except that one day the music might stop. I have trudged the steep hills of time, with life on my back like a burden, never thinking the work of living might end. And I have sat by rivers of hope, watching for my chance to come, watching my years float away. We are all stories in search of an ending. We are all prayers being answered. We are all the truth we tell. Our lives are change embodied. Only love stands still in the wind, unchanged by the weather of the heart, a love so certain and so pure, it knows no limit or season.

June 5

The moon and I are old friends. She has watched over me since I was a child. How many secrets we have shared I cannot count, how many flights to faraway lands, how many dreams followed late into the night. She has been there when I kept watch over those in hospital rooms or stood beneath the Alaska sky wondering what tomorrow might bring. She is the serenity of God, the image of a holy love that never sleeps. So if you are ever in need, awake in the quiet hours with your own thoughts, step out to stand in silver light, look up and whisper what you will, and I will know and join you in prayer, for the moon and I are old friends.

June 6

An open mind, a caring heart, a generous spirit: the qualities of a spiritual life are not difficult to achieve. These three simple virtues are each a step toward a life lived in faith. To be open to new ideas, to welcome diversity, to be curious in pursuit of wisdom. To be compassionate to all living things, to practice kindness, to be aware of the needs of others. To share what you have, to use your talents, to give freely to help your community. It does not take a scholar or a saint to learn these lessons, it only takes the intention of a pure soul set on the course to heaven. Live these three each day and you will find the peace you seek and the love you deserve.

June 8

Light the fire of your language, O God, and let it speak in every land, words of peace in war torn places, words of mercy in places of such sorrow, words of hope in places filled with dark corners. Give us all your Spirit of love that we may have the courage and wisdom to listen to one another, to hear what must be said, to speak the truth, to teach our children, to proclaim a new beginning for every living thing. Get us up out of our closed rooms of culture, out into the marketplace of thought, the corridors of power, the halls of justice. Let your light shine so brightly it reveals the beauty of your diversity, the joy of your voice delighting in us all.

June 9

Have met many angels in my time, good people who were suddenly given a task by God to perform, people who were at the right place at the right time, who showed up to help, who saved the day, who turned the wheel of life in the right direction. They have been nurses and teachers, friends and strangers, young and old, but always agents of grace, the embodiment of kindness, the proof that goodness is still alive and well in the world around us. I thank God for these angels of the everyday, saints of the common light who are our neighbors and our companions on the road to healing and hope. Bless you,

June 10

They say as you get older you get more set in your ways. That's alright with me. I am getting set in my ways. In fact I am getting downright stubborn. I refuse to believe that greed will triumph over justice, that racism is an incurable social disease, that hunger and poverty cannot be overcome, or that our planet cannot be restored to its beauty as a garden of life. I am stubborn in my faith and optimism. I am tenacious in love, constant in compassion, unwavering in my ability to laugh, especially at myself. I hope many of you are getting set into these ways too. Let us be the curmudgeons of joy.

June 11

Close the mind that knows your heart, as close as your own breathing. Wherever you are, whatever your need, the mind of God is there, thinking it through with you, sorting out the tangles, looking for solutions. God is more than a source of warm comfort, though that is what we often want. God is also a keen intellect, a deep imagination, looking with you into the fog of choices to catch a glimpse of a thought not expected. Turn to this architect of our reason when you have cause, ask your questions, seek your answers. God will work with you as a trusted counselor should: one idea at a time until the puzzle fits.

June 12

There is an island to which you can go, a safe haven in a storm tossed sea, that will welcome you in peace beneath bright skies, and let you rest if even only for a while. The grace of God creates islands for us all, small sanctuaries when we need them. I have come to know mine well, a place to which I can return when I need, as calm a spot as any I could ever have imagined. I pray that you will come to know your quiet harbor too, that it will restore you, renew you, and give you time to regain your energy. Sail on as long as you like, brave the weather of life with courage, but when you need, come back to your island home. Your spirit knows the way.

June 13

I had another one of my dreams. In this one I ran a pawn shop for feelings. People would come in and leave their worries. I would loan them whatever currency they needed: patience, hope, humor, insight. Whatever they thought they could use. The nice thing about the dream was that no one ever came back to get their worry. They used what they borrowed and found what they needed. Of course, we may feel we have some worries too big to pawn, but in my experience, God is always willing to receive them in exchange for grace. Take your worry to God in prayer and see if what you receive can help. That shop is open twenty-four hours a day.

June 15

Look again with the eyes of your spirit, turn to see the world around you, not cast in shadow but light, not closed with walls of stone, but open to the morning air of a new dawn. Look again with the vision God gives you, a free soul rising up to behold the path to heaven, a way walked by many before you, a bridge over sea and sky, a land where dreams are as common as birds. You were born to see what is now and what is coming to be. You have the gift of spiritual sight. Look up, look out, look again, and claim the blessing you see so clearly before you.

June 16

Let your dreams drift down like falling snow, a thousand hopes caught on the wind, the silent proof of who you are, the wisdom you wear like old shoes. You began your dream walk when you were only a child. You imagined a world that others could never see. Now you have answers within you that many prayers are seeking. Let your truth risk the light of day. Speak what you feel, what you know, what you have lived. Now is the hour for your witness, the moment for your voice to be heard. You have waited for this for longer than you can remember. Speak your truth and break the bonds others believed could never be broken. Speak and be free.

June 17

I have been stringing together quiet spaces in my life like pearls. I create five minute silent spaces wherever I am. I just stop what I am doing, sit if I can, or stand apart a little from those hurrying past me. I take a moment to look at what is around me, to breathe in and breathe out, to be fully aware of where I am. These time spaces are not deep meditation or prayer. They are only windows. They show me what I am seeing. They show me who I am in the midst of my life. They slow me down. They open my mind and heart. They are a rosary of mindfulness. With them I count my blessings. Through them I learn the contentment of just being me.

June 18

We may think we have very little to offer, but that is not really true. We have more love in us than we could ever possibly give away in one lifetime. We have enough compassion in our hearts to embrace the whole world, if only we could reach that far. We have a million chances to spend time with a child or with an elder, a million kind words we could say to lift up another soul. We are abundant in mercy, rich in understanding, gifted at listening which is so often all that people need for us to do. We are all more than able to support justice, bring peace, embody hope. We have so much to offer, so much to give in making this life a joy for others

June 19

God watch over all who keep a quiet vigil this day, all of us who have unanswered prayers, deep hopes, private longings. Look into our souls and read the handwriting of our hearts, the messages we would share only with you. So often we run out of words, dear God. We have thought our way to a place deeper than reason where only our feelings speak in a silent language. We cannot fully explain or describe anymore. We just stand before you, opening our lives into your care, trusting that your Spirit will know what we need without words. Have mercy, dear God, this day on all of us who have moved as far as we can to reach your loving hand.

June 20

Maybe it is the monk in me, or maybe it is the teacher, but of the three disciplines we should keep in a practical spiritual life, the one we often neglect is the study of holy writing. We do our work, sometimes more than we should. We do worship, sometimes less than we should. But we do not do the holy homework monastic saints like St. Benedict tell us is essential for a balanced spiritual life. Let me encourage us to be intentional about our learning. Spiritual life is continuing education. We always have more to read, to study, to discover. Wisdom is not often given, it is what we gain when we strive to understand.

June 22

Last night I sat again with my Spiritual Mother, an elder of great honor in my Native nation. Her grace and wisdom reminded me how important it is that we show respect to those who walk before us on the journey of life. I believe any culture can be blessed by the vision of its older women and men. I pray, therefore, for every person who has crossed the bridge of time to reach an older age. May you have health, peace, and love. And may you sit in the center of the circle, the hoop of your nation, telling your stories as signposts for others to follow as we all continue along the path our ancestors traced so well and so long ago.

June 23

Let it begin with me, the coming of kindness into the world around me. Let me be a bridge to bring light into my community, a healing light to warm young and old alike. I know that each one of us has the capacity for goodness, the instinct to help, the wisdom to create what is missing. It begins here, with each of us, within each of us, that natural impulse to have faith in tomorrow, to have the will to change. Let it begin with me: that is all we need to unlock the door of mercy, to free caged dreams, to set the sails of the soul to catch a fresh wind. Let it begin with me, with you, with all of us who are willing to risk what is for the sake of what might be.

June 24

I drove around an old lake, a quiet lake surrounded by tall trees, in a late afternoon when the sun was drifting toward the horizon and the dark clouds were gathering to welcome the night with rain. I looked across the still water. I breathed in the sense of peace that was nothing more than the natural world slowly going about its business of beauty. Even in the most difficult times, the most hectic times, we are embraced by the endless cycles of life around us. We are held in the palm of peace, if only we look to see it. I pray a quiet lake in your life, the scent of rain in the distance, the evening and the day dancing gently to the music of the wind.

June 25

I watch the ever flowing stream of stories, sliding past me on the electronic river, images of lost girls and falling bombs, floods and famines, the starving poor and the indolent rich, all passing in little pieces of digital dots, streaming, video snips, a history of life compressed into a twitter. Our age can keep us informed but teach us very little. The attention span of the eye and heart become abbreviated. The next story always on the feed. Hold steady the vision of my faith, O God, freeze frame the reality. Do not let me drift on emotional autopilot. Shatter the pixel wall between me and my human family. Let me feel what I see.

June 26

K indle again the fires of your bright spirit, let the energy within you run like liquid light through your soul. You were made to create, to discover, to express yourself in ways known only to you. You have a language of visions within you, a chronicle of all that you have seen and understood. Let those words weave their charm of wisdom, opening up your heart to touch a hundred more hearts, inspiring others to stand beside you, minds uplifted, eyes turned to the source of light itself. Kindle again the fires of your bright spirit, for this is your time to shine, your moment to carry an eternal flame to the high hearth of heaven.

June 27

M any years ago, when I was out on Kodiak Island in Alaska, a little girl asked me if her kitten that had just died would go to heaven. Without a moment's hesitation I replied "of course your little kitten will go to heaven" and I meant it. I still do. In Native tradition we believe all life is sacred. Everything God created was made in love and they are all beloved of the Great Spirit. What a sterile heaven it would be without birds singing in the trees or dogs running through the fields. Today I remember in prayer all of our animal friends who have gone before us. Blessed be all God's creatures, great and small, now and forever.

June 29

I am never alone, for wherever I go the Spirit seems to follow like a shadow, a quiet presence in all seasons, sharing in joy or sorrow, a wise counselor, a strong friend, a source of energy for the work that must be done. I believe we all have this same access to spiritual companionship in our lives. We are not solitary creatures, left to struggle our way through hardships, but active builders of our daily lives, partnered with the Spirit, given a chance to do together what we might never accomplish alone. We have the help of God every day. We have all the tools we need. No task is too great, no blessing beyond our reach, no love we cannot give.

June 30

How beautiful you are, O God, in all the places I find you. I see you in the early morning, when the birds first wake the sun, waiting patiently for me in the garden, as fresh and green as new life can be. I watch you gather up your billowing skirts in clouds of gray and black, flashing out streamers of light like ribbons from your hair. I meet you in the twilight, walking so softly beneath the trees, a quiet whisper of your breath to move the leaves along the path. How beautiful you are, in all the ways I see you, in every season and every hour. Let me see you always, O God, for as long as I live, as though it were for the very first time.

J U L Y

July 1

Sometimes I wish there was a delete button for parts of my past. When I think about the things I have done, the mistakes I have made: it would be so good to just stop remembering them. Even better would be the chance to go back and re-write my own history. But my life is not a computer. No delete or reset buttons. Nothing so automatic. Dealing with the past takes time, prayer and patience. I ask for forgiveness. I work on change. I strive toward the good. I count on grace. I turn with God in a new direction. Memory remains but hope arrives. I guess healing is old school. It takes a while, but when it comes, it lasts forever.

July 2

I have decided to do some time traveling. I am a little too accustomed to this time frame. It is time for a change. So I will travel in time by giving some of my time away. I will find someone who could use a little extra, an elder who would like to talk, a child who would like to play, a friend who would like to get a call, a group that could use an extra hand: I will find the destination for my experiment and give them as much of my time as I can. And by doing this, I will actually move from one place to another. I will move from this reality to a happier reality, to a place of smiles, to a sense of satisfaction at having made someone else's time more meaningful.

July 3

I have missed more than I have found, looking back it seems that way. How quickly the days run like children chasing one another down the hill, as evening comes to the park. I am older now so I notice the shadows more. How poignant the passing of a young couple walking into twilight. Calm the night coming with its velvet cape of stars, calm the older heart listening to the distant sounds of laughter. What we miss does not outweigh what we gain, when we let the balance find its own measure. Love is in the sunset as surely as in the dawn. Grace sits beside us, on the park bench, until the fireflies remind us that it is time to go home.

July 4

Open your heart, faithful watcher, receive the vision you have waited so long to see. You have kept your mind alert to possibilities others could not see. You have let your hopeful imagination consider new ways to solve old problems. And all the while you have been alone in your vigil while others were laboring away in the empty fields below. But now the light of insight breaks the far horizon. The proof of what you believed is at hand. Your witness will become a blessing, your tenacity a virtue, your patience a reward. Time has turned events to where you thought they would be, rejoice and release the healing you have intended all along.

July 6

There is no age to love, for love is timeless, even when the years carry us season by season, from first flowers to first snowfall, love remains within us as new as the look across a room that took our breath away, and leaves us still wondering how we could ever feel so happy, so certain, so unafraid to take life up in our arms and dance the night away. Love is God's gift against all doubts and reasons, a bright blessing of hope amid the ashes, a beginning that never ends, love is the spirit that keeps us young, as young as the God who makes each day and sends it spinning out into the sunlight, as if it were the first day of forever.

July 7

I know that it can't always be easy for you. I know that you have a great many things on your mind, more probably than you let on about. But I want to take only a moment to say that I respect you for what you are doing. To be a person of faith, to reach out to help others, to remain hopeful even in the face of difficult odds: that takes character. That takes courage and integrity. I have seen that in you, and I know I am not alone. Others see it too. In fact, they count on it. And most of all, God sees it. Every day, quietly, God watches over you, blessing the difference you are making in this world and keeping you safe for the world to come.

J u l y 8

I pray a simple joy into your life, a small blessing unexpected. If I had the ability I would lift every care from your shoulders, let you walk free of worry, but neither you nor I can stand apart from the fragile fact of our lives. We are made of clay and to clay we will return. But between then and now what a sweet song we can sing, ringing the earth with the gladness of every day, taking joy and giving joy, passing on the hope that set us free, embracing life as if it were an old friend come home at last, never to wander again. Watch your heart's horizon. The blessing I send will come when you least expect, but most need: a simple joy into your life.

J u l y 9

I was laughing about something I heard recently. A man said: it is good to keep an open mind, but not so open that your brains fall out. Now that is funny, especially for someone like me who likes to think of himself as open-minded. It got me to thinking. Being open to new or different ideas is one thing, but being so open that you have no strong stand to take on any issue is another. The man's joke helped me to do a little inventory of what I really believe. It brought me to think about what I value. I still want to keep an open mind, but I want to balance that with a clear sense of what I hold sacred. Sometimes funny is wise.

July 10

Here is a prayer for an unknown friend. I send it out and trust that the Spirit will bring it to the right person. I am not sure who that is, but I know that somewhere out in this wide world, perhaps nearby or maybe on the other side of midnight, there is a human being in need of prayer. I know this because I have been there. I have had moments when I wondered if anyone cared. In times like that it would have been so good to know that someone was praying for me. So I send out my own prayers now to find an unknown friend. I hope you will join me. O God, give this blessing to whoever needs it most. Please let them know they are not alone. Amen.

July 11

One of the nice things about getting older is that the list of possible temptations seems to get a little shorter. When I was younger there seemed to be a lot more options. So I have decided to offer this GET OUT OF ONE TEMPTATION FREE card. If you are like me and don't have the energy to rob a bank, it may help with some of the smaller temptations. If you are facing one of the bigger ones, I hope it will be a gentle reminder to back away slowly and find your joy in freedom. And I end with a prayer for us all, at any age, who live in a world that constantly urges us to take the shortcut: may we stay on our path toward all that is good.

July 13

Help is on the way. Faster than you can say amen, she rises on mighty wings, moving through the air like a great ship, racing through the clouds, uncaring for the weather, no storm can touch her, no tempest delay her, no force on Earth able to slow her determined power, with those wings like sails, eyes like lights against the dark, steady and certain, moving toward you without relent, coming to answer your call, able to hear even a single quiet voice amid all the voices swirling on the streets, see how quickly she comes, coming to be by your side, to help you, to guard you, coming to love you, look up, see, she is already here.

July 14

Prayers for all young lives just starting, for every new heart just beginning to beat the rhythm of life, the joyous sound of hope when the world seems so big and the chances seem so many. God watch over our youth, our children, our infants still in arms. God watch over couples just learning to run side by side along the open lanes of love. I celebrate all of these fresh faces in our universe, these sources of energy, moving creation forward, making the music the stars wait so patiently to hear. Protect all young lives, O God, help them over the rough spots, show them the way, give them the visions we older spirits still dream.

July 15

One of the most precious things we will ever have in this life is trust. It is more valuable than any material possession we own. And yet, we can never keep it for ourselves. If we try to horde it, it goes away. We can have it only if we share it. Giving our trust to another is offering them a part of who we are. It is the most intimate exchange we will ever make. I know many of us have tried to make this exchange and been hurt when our trust was broken. If this has happened to you, turn to the One who will never let you down. God can restore what you have lost, so you may trust again, and love again, without fear or hesitation.

July 16

You are the love some other heart seeks, you are the healing some wounded life needs. You are hope for some broken spirit, you are peace for some frantic mind. We are each the answer to some prayer, some need, some longing. We do not have to be heroic or wise to fulfill this role. We only have to be ourselves. We only have to be faithful. In the economy of God, even a small gift can become a great blessing, even a single person can save a community. Be aware of who you are. Recognize the authority residing in your word. Take the chance to be your calling, share who you are, and watch light flow into the world around you.

July 17

How many times have I come to pray for peace in the Middle East, O God? More times than I can remember. It may be that you are tired of hearing my same lament, my same appeal, my same hope, but I am sorry because there is nothing else I can do. Even if my prayer rug is old and frayed by now, still I will come before you to bend the knee and ask for the peace of Jerusalem. I make no distinctions between races or religions or nationalities. I ask for justice for every person alike and seek their common safety, their right to live. We cannot seem to solve this sadness, but you can. Please, let the time be now. Work your miracle for mercy's sake.

July 18

I have seen you again tonight in my prayers. You stand there, in my mind's eye, just beyond the candlelight. I am not sure why. I am not sure what your presence means, other than it is a sign that you are waiting for something. I have trusted my instinct and turned my prayers toward you. I have asked for you to feel the power and love of God in your life. I have asked for the Spirit of grace to come to you and give you what you most need at this moment in your journey. I have cast my prayer around you like a wreath of light. I saw your image fade when the candle went out, but I know my prayer will remain, a blessing made, a promise kept.

July 20

I would like to take a spiritual selfie of this community. I am so proud of what we have become. We are a small proof that religion does not have to be a cause for the negative things people associate with it. We are all different. We do not come from the same faith tradition. We have as many opinions as there are people listed as "friends". And we are friends. We treat one another with respect. We listen to what the other has to say. Even if we do not agree, we pray for one another out of genuine kindness and compassion. I wish I could clone you all. I am grateful for the quiet witness we make to hope. I pray our light may continue to shine.

July 21

Today I will be at a shelter, praying with women who need a safe place to heal. Please, God, let my prayers be as strong as ever. Let them reach out to comfort and support, protect and defend, nurture and uphold, renew and restore. Let me stand with my sisters in humility, for they have much to teach me. And make me a witness to justice, an advocate for an end to the violence, that pulls apart hearts and homes, scattering the hope of our children. Let me speak up, speak out, speak a love that ends the hidden harm endured by so many. Help me to help, good God, these brave spirits and gentle souls.

July 22

I was thinking about how our emotions are like old friends. We know them very well. They have been part of our lives for years. And sometimes we know when they will be coming around, we are expecting them. But other times, they just show up, and not always at a good time. Anger comes to mind. There are times when I am glad anger has arrived. When I am confronting an injustice, then it is very helpful to have anger on my side. But other times, when I am dealing with a crabby clerk at the store or a fussy child, anger is not who I need at all. Then compassion would be nice to see. If I can choose my friends, let me choose them wisely.

L et this quiet prayer come to you, wherever you may be. Let it come in gently, without fanfare or announcement, like a breeze slipping through a window, a soft reminder of the movement of life around you. Let it be a comfort, a comfort because at times we need that calming of life, that sense that somehow things will be alright. Nothing dramatic, nothing strident, just a feeling that you are cared for, watched over, supported in what you must do each day. Let this quiet prayer be all of those things for you, because you have carried your burdens and helped so many others: let this be your time, your moment to know that you are beloved of God.

July 24

Here comes change again, that persistent visitor to my well-ordered world, showing up unexpected, turning over my best laid plans, adding yet another problem on my plate. Take a number, I want to shout, I've got enough things to handle as it is. But change doesn't care. It just laughs and starts rearranging the furniture. There are days when I would be glad for a little monotony, some of the same old same old, nothing much happening at all. But God has a way of keeping things interesting, so I will get used to change and not complain. At least, not much. I still think a few quiet days to cope with what I've got would be nice. But change has a better idea.

I feel the healing again, beginning to move around me, like troubled waters, a ripple of energy moving out from the center, the breath of God moving over the water, the energy of the Spirit riding the wind. Over the years I have come to feel when it is beginning, this flow of healing power that will circle those in need, touching them unseen, restoring their minds and bodies. It is a wonderful outpouring of hope. A blessing of renewal that cannot be denied or stopped. It moves, like waves, like air, like the force of life that knows no barrier or boundary. Be alert, be open, for the healing is coming again, a gift for any who will receive it.

July 27

I sing a joy into your life, here at the midnight hour, chanting quiet prayers beneath the moon. I have no gift to give but kindness, no wisdom but compassion, no authority but our shared experience. Like you I have watched the seasons turn, deep cycles of change, blessings and sorrows mixed in the many colors of our lives. What is spiritual is what is most ordinary, the common threads of hope and mercy, the things we know best because we have lived them all. So I chant the turn of another day, spinning grace into the world, praying joy into your life, only a small token, but one that I know you will always remember.

July 28

Blessed days passing by, like shadows running over the fields, cast by clouds on a windy day, racing to find the horizon. How quickly the life we share moves from moment to moment. We are time travelers, you and I, journeying without ceasing the hours of our own awareness. We collect memories like flowers along the way, faded reminders of love shared and sorrow spent, learning our lessons as fast as we can. We are not alone in wishing we could linger, all our family flies beside us, swift along the currents of change. But what a comfort to carry eternity in our pocket, the day to come when we will know no parting.

July 29

Be renewed in your spirit now: let this prayer lift you up, let it restore your strength and your energy, filling your soul with fresh hope, opening your vision to see the wonder that is your life. Be renewed in every part of your life: in mind and body and faith, so that the heaviness of your labor grows light, the waiting passes quickly, the problems suddenly seem so much smaller. Be renewed in your heart: knowing that the Spirit is with you, that angels walk beside you, that God is opening doors and calling you to follow. This is the time of your next birth, the passing from gray to light, the touch of a holy hand that will empower you with its anointing.

July 30

Bend your heart toward love, as a flower bends to face the sun. When all is said and done, the only true measure of our lives is how well we loved. How well we gave love, received love, shared love, defended love, created love. No other honors or accolades will matter when the dry wind blows from the south to sweep our memory clean, only the love we were will linger, only love will still speak our name in the hearts of those we embraced with its purity. We were made to love, you and I, made by the author of love, made in the image of love, to have the courage and the strength to live our love, to be the love we are.

July 31

God, let me speak plainly in this prayer. Like so many others, I have watched the spread of violence in recent days. Planes and bombs falling from the air, the assault of troops over borders, the threats of terror in towns and cities. If this madness cannot be stopped, then at least shelter the innocent from harm. Stretch out your right hand and protect the elders and children who are trapped in the crossfire. Do not let the innocent suffer. Gather up the young mothers and babies under your wing. Call the grandparents into your watchful care. Cover the hospitals with your left hand. Whatever is yet to come, hold these lives precious and secure.

AUGUST

August 1

Golden the light that comes before you, bright the promise of your dreams. You are a mystic by intuition, a person who senses the reality behind reality, the unseen movement of grace that shapes the lives we lead. Your prayers have shown you the mysteries of God, the quiet ways in which prayers are answered, and those prayers have touched many people for whom you care, your kindness has carried healing to many hearts. None of this has gone unnoticed. Even if you never say a word about it, the eye that never sleeps has watched the goodness within you, and now turns to bless you for your faithfulness. Golden is the light before you.

August 3

I believe there is a peace that is within each of us, a still center like a quiet pool. It often gets lost in the press of daily worries and the deep struggles we face with our lives. Illness obscures it, anxiety obscures it, anger obscures it: but that does not mean it is not still there. I believe this calm center to our lives is where the best part of ourselves, our innocence and goodness, remains at rest. It is where God resides within us, the source of our true strength and wisdom. I hope that you will share my faith in this sanctuary of the soul. I hope you will find your way there whenever you are in need. Let my words be a light for you on your path to peace.

A u g u s t   4

It is not easy to be strong in life, even if we understand what that really means. To be resilient in facing difficulties, to be undaunted by disappointments, to remain hopeful even against great odds: the definitions of spiritual strength vary, but the one thing that is common among us all is the fact that it is not something we can do alone. We need one another. We need support and nurture and understanding and fresh perspectives. We need community. If there is one spiritual thing we can all do, it is to offer our strength to help others. We can each build community. We can make it a little easier to be strong by being strong together.

A u g u s t   5

A night prayer. I stand beneath the stars and lift my heart to pray, please God I know that many others are awake tonight and awake for many reasons. Be with them all in their time of need. Keep them safe. Comfort them. Bring them to the new day they long to see. I know many others are sound asleep. Let them sleep in peace. Watch over them. Hold them. Let them awake to find you waiting on a bright and beautiful morning. I know there are others praying with me in these quiet hours. Hear our words however we say them and by whatever name we know you. Let there be as many blessings as the stars beneath which we pray.

August 6

What is that divine spark we call imagination? Last night I gathered with a small community of Native elders and scholars. I listened to their stories and heard wisdom in their words, I looked into their faces and saw tradition in their eyes. Today we will work to create something of lasting value for generations to come, a celebration of the Native story, a glimpse of God walking with our People. What a gift it is when we work together, wonder together, weave thoughts together. The Spirit has given us the ability to not only see what is, but what is coming to be. The joy of heaven is when we use that vision and dream a truth as yet unseen.

August 7

Give all that you can and gladly. Give your time to those for whom even a few minutes of companionship is a joy, give your kindness to those who may need a little grace in their lives, give patience to the one who is not easy to be around. Give to elders, give to children, give to the poor, give to the affluent. Give mercy, give love. Let these gifts of compassion come from you as freely as you can. Don't hold back. Let your love flow out like a small river finding its forest, like a stream rushing to look around the corner. There are few blessings in life greater than a generous spirit. It is the gift we give to ourselves when we give to others.

A u g u s t 8

Sometimes I think if I have no other spiritual skill, at least I have the gift to listen. It is not as easy as it sounds. I have to pay attention to the reality around me, be aware of the many layers of that reality, take nothing at face value, be discerning in my own prejudices as well as in the agendas being pushed toward me. I have to be patient, open minded and at the same time, critical in my thinking. I need to understand my own social and cultural location. I have to educate myself when there are subjects with which I am not truly familiar. Spiritual listening is not an exercise in being polite. It is growing in wisdom through faith and change.

A u g u s t 1 0

Tonight I focus every prayer, every thought, every hope on peace. I think of all those whose lives are in peril, people caught in the firestorms of war, villages and towns swept away by violence, ancient hatreds fueled by modern ambitions, intolerance and cruelty dancing amid the smoke, the crackle of gunfire an evil laugh in the distance. Come God of peace, come and stand in the midst of this madness, stretch out your great arms of love and still the winds of senseless sorrow. I cry out tonight with all the faith I have: let there be peace in the world, peace on the Earth, peace among your children by whatever name you call them.

A u g u s t 1 1

It is for the small things that we can be grateful, the many little blessings that surround us each day: simply waking up to a new morning, laughing with an old friend, watching a child take its first steps out into the world, seeing the clouds change shape beneath the sheltering sun. There are so many of these moments of grace, they float past us like colored leaves caught on the breeze, endless reminders of God's presence nearby, constant images of beauty and goodness. Even when we walk in the twilight of life, through the shadows that always come, they are lights along our path, blessed assurance to guide us to hope.

A u g u s t 1 2

I have not forgotten you. Over all these years, I have not forgotten you, but carried you with me, from place to place, from time to time, keeping you always in my memory, like a light I could not let fail, a sacred sign I could not lose. I admit that I shaped the memory. I let go of the tattered edges of the mistakes I made, the sorrows I caused, but kept the bright sounds of our laughter, the places we once walked, the feel of the air that preserves our past in its most perfect form. You have continued to bless me. That is how deep your memory runs, an ancient love forever young, a blessing without seasons. I have not forgotten. I will never forget. .

August 13

I would like to say a quiet word if I may. Recently our society has been shaken by the suicide of Robin Williams. There is a great deal being said about it, more than I can add to here, other than to wish him peace and pray comfort for those he left behind. My purpose is a little different. I would like to speak directly to any person who thinks they feel like Robin. I do this because in my community suicide is all too common. For Native people, Robin's death was not a shock, but a reminder. So here is my message to any who need it: You are not alone. You are loved. Talk to someone. Let the hurt out and God in. Give life one more chance. We need you.

August 14

Light the light of your heart and let it burn ever so brightly in these shadowed days. Your witness, our witness, the witness of all faithful people is needed now more than ever. Like candles coming alive in a dark corner, we need to shine forth hope and strength for a world bent by fear and bullied by war. Together we must believe that the simple goodness of common humanity is more powerful than the rants of angry minds. Let us now stand together, holding our lights of peace as high as we can, holding out the healing hand of shared love, singing the freedom of a new generation into life. Light the light of your heart and turn the night to day.

August 15

I am one of those people who likes to buy organic foods. I look for fruits, vegetables and other items that I think are grown as naturally as possible. The other day while I was grocery shopping it struck me that I feel the same way about my spiritual values. I like organic. I like my religion to be natural, simple, and without a lot of additives. I believe my faith should nourish me with the basic elements for a healthy spiritual life and not mask its flavor with a lot of sugar or disguise its intentions with misleading packaging. For me, faith is organic. It grows from the earth, from the rain, from the light of God. This matters because, after all, we are what we eat.

August 17

I believe in miracles, not only the big ones, but the small ones too. Like many of you, I can share a personal testimony to healing events that can only be described as miraculous. Some of those are dramatic moments of physical healing. They defy the odds and leave us without rational explanations. They are facts of faith for many of us. But just as important to me are the many other "miracles" I see: broken relationships being restored, unexpected love walking in the door, much needed funds suddenly appearing. The list is long. I do not claim that in every case God is micro-managing our lives. I just give thanks for them all, big and small.

August 18

I am going to have lunch today with one of my mentors. She is an elder among my people and for over forty years she has been my friend. She is a woman of strong character, deep wisdom and abiding faith. I believe we are all shaped by people like her, by the elders of our lives, the mentors who have been there through our years of change. Some may have been with us only a short time, others have traveled with us for a lifetime. None of us could be who we are without them. I offer a prayer of thanks to God for them all, each and every one. I honor them for their gift to us, the gift of themselves, the gift of a journey shared.

August 19

Let no harm come to the one for whom this prayer is meant. Shield them from any danger, retrieve them from any harm. Let your holy light be their protection, your great mercy their defender. No illness nor accident will befall them, no anxiety nor fear will assail them, but only the calm assurance of your love open before them, as though they saw a wide and placid sea. So this prayer becomes the eye of any storm. It encircles the one who is cherished, whether infant or elder, within the safety of angels, holding them secure against all alarms. Here these words, great God of peace, for in you is all our trust, our confidence and our devotion.

A u g u s t   2 0

I do not know if there is a saint who presides over common sense, but if there is I would surely ask him or her to step up the flow of this grace into the world, for it seems we have far too little to go around. No, we will not all finally agree on every issue and, yes, fighting one another to try to make it so is really pointless. No, there are no superior people with more of a claim to wisdom than others, and, yes, we have enough to share if only the few would not always need to have more. Our sad old world could be blessed with some common sense to help us find the peace and cooperation we so sorely need. That is a vision worthy of a saint.

A u g u s t   2 1

I bought a wooden top the other day, the kind you wind up with a string, toss and spin. I don't think they make them anymore, but in the early 1950's they were hi-tech toys for kids. That little top is a meditation in itself. It reminds me to go outside to play. It tells me that simple can be fun. It helps me to bring my values of the past with me into my future. It shows me that being by myself can be a good thing. It keeps my memory alive. It demonstrates that the kid in me is still there. It provides an exercise in either patience or pride depending on if I can get it to work. That top whispers truth as it spins my spirit on the balance of life.

August 22

What do we do when it feels like things are starting to fall apart? I don't ask this to make us anxious; I ask it because we are already anxious. I am not a big news watcher, but even a person with his head in the clouds as much as I can feel the impulse of fear spreading around the world. So I think it is time to come down to earth and proclaim again the intense power of love. Things are not falling apart. The world is not coming unglued. Our community is not overwhelmed. The love of God is the same love that we share with one another. It is what binds us together. And against it fear falls flat. Do not be anxious. Be love and be whole.

August 24

You have a vision no one else has seen. You have a unique experience of life, a rare insight into our shared reality. You have seen things, done things, felt things in a way unlike that of any other person on Earth. Therefore, your story is singular. No one else has lived it; no one else can tell it. Within that story there may be lessons vital to someone else, perhaps someone you know, perhaps someone living a thousand miles away you will never meet. You have the key. You have the answer. You have the one perspective that can change a human life. Maybe even a whole community. You are destiny for another. You are the truth of a lifetime.

A u g u s t   2 5

This prayer is said without words. It is for you, the quiet one. You are not a person who likes to take the stage. You don't feel the need to speak on every subject, have the last word, or run the meeting. You prefer to listen. You take in every word that flows around you. You do not rush to voice your opinions, but weigh what you hear on the scales of your own experience and conviction. You are not timid in what you believe just because you do not need to announce it, instead you are an anchor of faith among those who often drift with every new current of thought. I honor you for your discernment and wisdom, and bless you without speaking.

A u g u s t   2 6

I am in a canyon beside a still lake under the eye of a hot summer moon. This is Cheyenne and Arapaho country. The ancient spirit of these Native nations moves through the night, whispers of strength and wisdom, and lifts me up to pray with a pure heart for all who may be in need. Healing is in the air. Hope is moving across the land. The prayers I say tonight will be carried far and wide, helping those who are alone, who are struggling, who are seeking, who are recovering. Name them in your own heart and let these prayers find them, like arrows of light, flying through the darkness, flying under the eye of a hot summer moon.

August 27

Time to wake up. Time to let the spiritual alarm clock within my soul ring me into awareness. No more religion set on auto pilot. No more taking the impact of my values for granted. There are people around me I need to pay attention to, people waiting for me to notice them. There are new challenges to discover, new chances to practice what I preach. It is so easy to drift into the comfortable notion that I have learned all I need to be a person of faith, that I have arrived and can settle in to relax with God. Time to shake off the dust of my own privilege. Time to wake up, get up, and be active. Love now, sleep later.

August 28

In this lifetime we do not see the harvest of all we have planted. In fact, we may not even be aware that where we walked a garden will one day grow. Every act of kindness is a seed, every honest moment, every sacrifice, every generous sharing, they all scatter goodness and compassion around our lives, the countless seeds of hope caught on the breeze of the Spirit, sent out from each of us, known and unknown, intentional or accidental: the planting of a better world for those who come behind us. No, we may not see it all rise to bloom while we are here, but one day we will. We will see our harvest, fields of love, as far as the eye can see.

August 29

I love these quiet hours alone with God. They are monastic moments within my soul when I turn all of my life over to prayer and contemplation. I open my spirit to listen to what I need to hear, not the endless chatter of a noisy planet, but the still voice of an ageless wisdom. I share my prayers for all those I can name and for the countless others whose names I do not know, but whose human story is so much the same as mine. I read, I think, I wonder. I cannot now imagine a day without these holy times. And while I have no formula of faith for anyone else to follow, I like to believe others are as alone with God as me, each in their own way.

August 31

We are all jugglers. We have to manage our own internal lives, coping with our health and well-being. We have to care for our family and all of their ever changing needs. We are part of the greater community around us, being aware of our reality and responsive to it. It is not easy to do all these things at once. There are times when we can feel overwhelmed or tired. That is why we are given the help and support of the Spirit. God provides an extra pair of hands to keep our lives in balance and rhythm. You do not have to do it all. Handle what you can and entrust the rest to the One who would not let even a sparrow fall to the ground.

SEPTEMBER

September 1

Let me dance a little longer, before the music must stop. Let me feel the motion of life, the sway of life, out across the floor of the world, beneath the colored lights of heaven. Let me enjoy the night, feel the night, breathe in the stars and twirl around the sleepy moon. This dance you have given me is so precious, so wondrous and lyrical, let me dance just a little longer, gliding through time and space, turning with all of creation, turning and turning, as if there were no tomorrow. Then when the music must stop, we can go home. Then I will be happy to go home. I will dance home. Dance all the way home. With you. My God and my Maker.

September 2

I can understand why people go to fortune tellers and astrologers. So often our lives are like watching the tarot cards being dealt, we are never sure what the next card may bring. We seem to exist on the threshold of the unknown, walking the path between good news and bad. Two of the constants in life that we must cope with are uncertainty and ambiguity. I am not wise enough to tell you why this is so, but I am faithful enough to share in it with you, praying for both of us that we keep our balance, come what may, ready to embrace joy or face disappointment, living life to the full in the midst of change, letting love be our future no matter what.

September 3

One of the hardest things I have had to work on in my spiritual life is the idea that I can be forgiven. That is true for more people than me. We can become so accustomed to what we perceive as the unfairness of life, or so mesmerized by the gravity of our own mistakes in life, that we have trouble believing there can be true forgiveness in life. But God's grace is the counter balance to both of those assumptions. Life may be fickle, but God's mercy is constant. We can make serious mistakes, but reconciliation and restoration are ever present. Forgiveness is a healing force in our spiritual universe. It is there if we will only receive it.

September 4

Called out at night to be with a family in need, making the dash to the hospital, hurrying down empty halls, into rooms with anxious faces, bedside prayers measured out to the beep of medical machines. Home grateful all is well but with bleary eyed memories of so many other alarms answered, the priest in the firehouse of hope. So here is a prayer for the health of all who find these words: may the healing you most need, mind, body, or spirit, embrace you like a long lost friend, may you feel the change to strength flow through you like light, may you be at peace within the shelter of a love that never leaves you.

September 5

Come fly with me, out over the routine of cluttered time, away from the heavy footed sameness of caution, into the brisk air of the unplanned life, where anything might happen and usually does, where laughter comes quickly and joy is as catching as the common cold. Spread the wings of your imagination and together let us catch the current of the Spirit, the wind of a wilder season, carrying us far from our old familiar complaints toward a place we both know so well but have not yet seen. Be free with me, free to do what you spent your childhood dreaming, free to find the secret map to your heart, free to trust your soul to sing.

September 7

Be believing. Do not let the whispers of despair that drift through the dark clouds of chaos that surround us convince you that they are a voice of substance. Do not think that we are destined to walk into the night never to find another dawn. Be believing. Remember the strength that love has shown you in your own life. You are a witness to its truth, a living proof to how reality may be redeemed, hope may be restored, faith may be alive in joy. Be believing. Lift up your heart to see the vision you know is your future, not an end but a beginning, not sorrow but gladness. Be believing and let the light of who you are show others the way home. .\

September 8

We are all called, each in our own way, to do the work of creation, knitting together the many strands of grace that hold the universe together. We each have a task to perform, even if we are not always aware of its true purpose or intent. We may not even know what good we have done until the great cycles of love turn round and we discover the blessing we have been. We have moments when the curtain parts, we suddenly feel the cool air of heaven billowing about us, and for only an instant we know that we have made a difference. We are all called, called to be what no other can be, the handprint of our heart on the long walls of time.

September 9

Don't look back now, you have come this far, keep your eye fixed on the light before you, the single star just before twilight, the sign of your hope, seemingly still distant, but coming nearer every moment. Don't look back to past mistakes, old conflicts, memories that are like scars, but consider how much healing has already taken place in your spirit. You are so much stronger now, so much wiser, so much more at peace with the source of your blessing. Don't worry about what has been, but invite what is to come. You have a survivor's story you can tell, but you also have a dreamer's story yet to live: and that is an adventure you have just begun.

September 10

Now is the hour of our appeal, our common appeal raised in prayer by countless voices, rising up from every village and city, from all corners of our battered world, lifted up on the tired shoulders of the hungry and the poor, held up in the strong hands of working mothers and faithful fathers, spoken aloud in every language, a lament and a challenge, sent up to the silence of heaven, asking for peace, asking for an end to oppression and exploitation, asking for that ancient promise of a better tomorrow, when all the nations will rest from their anger, and all the wars will grow still, and all the children will come out, come out finally, to play.

September 11

Let love be your birthright for you are worthy of deep affection. You are a pure spirit of great value, a life to be treasured and respected. It does not matter if you have made mistakes, for so have we all, what matters is that you have sought to turn your heart to the good, giving what was entrusted to you, the kindness that changes lives, the patience that holds innocence forever. You are to be loved and told that you are loved, honored and cherished, held in the safety of arms that will never waver in their care for you. This is how you are known by the God who loves you and this is how you are known by all who see you through eyes of faith.

September 12

What spiritual language do you speak? How do you share what you believe in a way that others can understand and be blessed? We all have a language of our own, a gift for communicating our thoughts and feelings in ways that others can receive. Some of us speak with words, some of us speak through our art. Some of us speak the language of music, some of us speak through dance. Some let acts of service and compassion speak for them. Some can speak volumes without ever saying a word; they have the language of empathy. Whatever your language may be, use it, and let the truth you know be the message you share.

September 14

Do not be afraid, not of what is to come, or what has gone, of the unknown, or the known, of the remembered, or the forgotten, of the difficult, or the easy. Do not be afraid, not of illness, or grief, of loss, or gain, of not having enough, or having too much, of giving it away, or getting it back. Do not be afraid, of being alone, or being in the crowd, of not being seen, or being exposed, of being wrong, or being right, of not knowing, or knowing. Do not be afraid, of the stranger or the family, of the success or the failure, of winning or losing. Do not be afraid, of anything, anytime, anywhere, but rejoice, for God is ever beside you.

September 15

I will keep watch through each long night, guarding the sleep of the innocent, sheltering the dreams of the children, allowing the tired souls of hard working women and men to rest, keeping safe the homes of our elders. I will stay with the stars and chat to the moon, as I toss my silent prayers skyward, up into the high arc of heaven, naming those who need help, calling down swift-winged angels to make their healing rounds, keeping the vigil of peace for those sleepless under the threat of war. I will keep watch, expectant of the first light, knowing that it might be the one light, the coming of love, coming like dawn, never to leave again.

September 16

Sometimes I think the best measure of our spiritual lives is not our piety or charity, but our resilience. In our everyday lives, we weather many storms. There are always struggles and disappointments. We confront illness, financial troubles, family problems, issues at work or with friends. The list is endless and it is all just part of being alive. What gets us through these many challenges is not a goody-two-shoes spirituality that leaves us walking a few inches off the ground, but a good old-fashioned sense of joining hands with God and making it through to a better day. Spirituality is best if it works when you need it.

September 17

Everywhere I look I see the holy. In silent old trees watching over streets they have sheltered for generations, in clouds chasing one another across a gray sky full of the smell of rain, in a rocky seacoast where mystery follows the white spray of the sea beneath the gliding gulls: there I see the holy looking back through the eyes of Nature. In the bent hands of elders whose whole lives have been a story, in the darting figures of children flying across the afternoon grass: there I see the holy looking back through the eyes of humanity. All of the world, all of life, all of everything ever made by our God, is holy, and we are so blessed to be able to see it.

September 18

I have another modest proposal to make. Nothing too grand, just a simple notion that might prove helpful to anyone trying to live a more intentional spiritual life. My idea is this: declare one day a week as your slow day. The rest of the week, you can run along at the usual hectic pace of our generation, but give yourself and your family one day to move according to a much older clock. Take time for breakfast together. Walk somewhere instead of drive. Spend some time in the park or garden. Have a long cup of tea and a chat. Have a sit down dinner. Read before bed. Slow down for one day and give yourself time to just be you.

September 19

What witness will we make, in this troubled time, amid all the clamor and confusion, beneath the dark skies of war, when epidemics steal lives by the thousands, and the politics of power lead us in the spiral of pride? What will we say? What will we do? Each person must make his or her own answer, but I will say on behalf of all who will join me: we will not be passive in this hour, resigned to loss as though it defined us, but we will stand together, without regard to any divisions among us, and proclaim the peace of God as our sovereign hope, the rights of every human being as our claim, and love as our one and only ambition.

September 21

Please God, bless all those who have been so hurt by their community of faith that they feel they can never return; bless those who have been so steadfast in their faith that we would call them saints; bless the doubters who are not sure they can commit to a belief; bless the activists who are so motivated by what they believe that they take risks in your holy name; bless those who have just stepped over the threshold of faith for the first time; bless the wise elders of our communities who keep wisdom alive; bless the musicians and the singers who grace our worship. Please God, bless all your people, wherever they may be along the Way.

September 22

I stood with my son, deep in the tribal lands of our people, watching a great storm roll through the night, piercing the rain-swept skies with flashes of electric energy, booming out the drum beat of heaven's thunder. Generations of our ancestors seemed to ride the wild horses of the storm above us, racing across the clouds, trailing sheets of rain like blankets, crying out the ancient songs of generations gone by. The past is not distant. It is not a faded memory. The past lives around us every day, breaking into our lives with the light of memory, sounding the drum of tradition, calling us to what lies ahead. Our future is beyond the rain.

September 23

Hear now this healing word, sent out by the messenger who has known hurt himself. You will be well. Even if you must share your body with an illness, even if you have limitations, even if your recovery is as slow as seasons, you will be well. In your spirit you will feel it first, that sense of inner strength, that warm light from within. It will begin the healing deep in the center of your soul. Then your mind will recognize the signs of life, feel the renewal of your being, and turn to acknowledge the truth of your own healing. Then your body will be lifted up, held in great arms of comfort, and you will be well, well in every part of you, well and returned to joy.

September 24

I would never presume to think I could know the ultimate plan and purpose of God in creation, but I do think there are some clues that are hard to miss. Clue #1: All of the universe, from the smallest thing to the greatest, is filled with incredible diversity. There is not just one form to reality, but endless variations. Clue #2: Change is built in. Nothing stays the same, but always evolves into something new. Clue #3: Choice is the gift given to human beings. We cannot control anything, but we can make choices that make a difference. The spiritual lesson to consider: God desires diversity, embraces change, and gives us the choice to do the same or not.

September 25

Where is the source of your strength? What has sustained you through your most difficult days? Within each of us I believe there is a quiet place, a deep place, a place of the soul that is hallowed ground. It is where we keep our most precious memories. It is where we look into the mirror of time and see ourselves as we have been through all of our years. It is a sanctuary where only we can go, but when we are there, where we know we are not alone. Where is the source of your strength? Let your answer be a blessing. Whatever you face, you do so with an authority both ancient and eternal, a covenant of love that can never be broken.

September 26

Time to let go for a while, let the worries I have held so tightly in my hands float up to heaven like so many brightly colored balloons, let the frustrations I have known fall from my fingers like confetti, let the weight around my shoulders sprout wings and lift me off this troubled sphere, up and out into cleaner air, where only birds and prayers fly among the clouds. I have stood my post. I have been diligent and serious and caring. Now it is time to let go, for a while, a while of laughter and music, of candlelight and starlight and all the lights Japanese lanterns can muster to make my backyard a palace by the sea. Yes, it is time to let go.

September 28

Bind my heart to your will, O God, and let me always follow where you lead. Take away any pride that tempts me from obedience and give me humility when I come before you. Help me again to see the strength in serving others, the authority in coming last, the wisdom in listening before I speak. Keep my spirit balanced between the courage it needs to face what comes and the peace it needs to do so in confident joy. You are the source of all I have, of all that I am and ever will be. You are my pledge of hope and my dream of justice. Bind my heart to your will, O God, and let my life bear witness to your endless love.

September 29

The good that you do is not constrained by time, but lives on like an echo throughout many lifetimes yet to come. Your deeds, your choices, your witness touches other lives, spreading out, moving out, like a network of light, inspiring, healing, changing those around you, often those who are far beyond even your own awareness. You are the center of a great wheel of love, a wheel that never ceases to turn and whose spokes touch the edges of history. Do not think of yourself as small and inconsequential, but celebrate the fact that God has put you where you are for a purpose. Your life is not a candle, but a star.

September 30

For many years I lived the life of a teacher. I lived in academic communities. I learned first-hand how enriching, how life changing a school experience can be. I also witnessed other moments when the balance between Boards, faculty, students and administrators spun out of control. Our schools in this country are under enormous pressure. They are over-extended, under-funded, and often neglected. Students take on crippling debt just to complete their education. Teachers are asked to do more with less. Knowing all of this as intimately as I do, I pause to pray for our schools: may the Spirit of wisdom watch over them all.

OCTOBER

October 1

With God, there are no deadlines, for that I am very grateful. We live in a world of time limits, limited offers, expiration dates, cut off points. And yet, our lives rarely work that way. They are not always so neat and tidy, running by the precision of a stop watch. Things come up, things change. We get distracted by other needs, called away suddenly to take care of other business. And truthfully, we sometimes put things off, afraid to face them, living in denial. The wonderful grace of God is that there is always an eleventh hour for mercy. Forgiveness is available long past the date when we should have asked for it. God's love is open all night.

October 2

Like many of you there are times when I have to face difficult medical issues. This is one of those times. I am keeping watch over my mother who is in the hospital. Given our situation, I may not be able to write as usual. But I certainly will be praying. I believe at moments like this, we are nearer to God than ever. So I take this as an opportunity to focus my spirit and my love toward all of you who, like my own mother, may be in need of healing. My prayers will be rising through this night for you. They will encircle you. May the gentle Spirit of healing be with you, may you feel that Spirit, and may you be healed in every way. Amen.

October 3

When the power of love is released through prayer, it does not matter how the prayer is said, or who says the prayer, or what culture they inhabit. It only matters that the words, spoken or unspoken, rise from the heart of a longing soul to touch the intention of God. When that connection is made, when that ancient bond is invoked, then a force is released that cannot be denied. Prayer works. It changes lives. It restores the world. It heals and blesses. It opens doors to wisdom. Thank you all for your prayers. I am honored to stand with you as a people without borders: we care enough for one to pray for all.

October 5

Arise into your true calling, lifted up by the challenge that stirs the imagination. You were made for this, you were born to this, shaped by a lifetime of experience to be the one who could do it. In each of us there is a sense for what we are called to do, an awareness of the mission that guides our life's purpose. Even if we wander in other directions, we often feel called back to this path. We are sealed in the Spirit to our vocation, stewards of the gifts we are given. Be blessed again into your talent. Be proud of your vision. Arise into your true calling, becoming the creative person you were meant to be, the sign of hope you embody.

October 6

Gladden the hearts of your people, O God, and let them feel confident that you are still near to them. Warm the hearts of your people, and let them trust one another with a trust that is returned and genuine. Strengthen the hearts of your people, and let them stand up in unity against every challenge. Comfort the hearts of your people, let them discover the clear water of healing and the still water of peace. Open the hearts of your people, O God, let them build your city without walls but with streets wide in welcome to every stranger. Listen to the hearts of your people, let their every breath be a prayer of praise to you.

October 7

The other day I mentioned to someone that I was thinking of finding a part time job at a local Jamba Juice to help make ends meet. I thought it good work for an old guy like me to mix up fruit juice drinks, a lot easier than moving furniture. In fact in my life I have moved furniture, driven trucks, cleaned tables and done the night shift in a warehouse, among other things. So I take a moment to honor every woman or man who knows what it means to put in a hard day's work for an honest wage. It is not always easy. You don't get paid what you deserve. But there is dignity in honest labor and I pray a blessing on every person who understands what I mean.

October 8

I know there is more than a little of the mystic within you. You have lived on the wilder shores of faith, along the rocky coast of polite religion, where visions can roll in like storms, and the Spirit can move like a strong wind from the sea. There is more the scent of wood smoke around you than incense, something older, something from the Earth, a faith that has deeper roots, an ancient memory that remembers the source of wonder. There is more than a little of the prophet within you, the quiet word of what is coming, the kind word of what it means, the word of wisdom to spin another dream from the pale light of the moon.

October 9

How strange it is that so many people seem to want to define their religion by drawing out its boundaries and then guarding their frontiers so only those who agree can enter in to claim a place among the chosen. How much better to live in a faith without any boundaries at all. My spirituality is an open field. It looks out to an endless sky. It allows anyone access if they share a curiosity to know more, to do more, to enjoy more of what we call faith. I am not anxious that people agree with me. I think houses of God should not be bunkers, but meadows, with room for children to play, and room for seekers to breathe.

October 10

The image of the group hug often gets a grin from us. It seems funny, but oddly enough it came to my mind when I had to deal with one of life's most common emotions: disappointment. Like most of our feelings, disappointment comes in different sizes. There are small versions, which we get over quickly, and very large impacts that can leave a soul scar forever. Disappointment is lost hope. It is the eternal what if, the sense of what might have been or should of been, but never will be. It is a dream dissolved right before us. So for all of us who have known this feeling, great or small, here is a collective hug of recognition and support.

October 12

I stood before a new world in the making, people of every faith drawn together by a shared vision, a hope for peace, a dream of justice, a witness to love more ancient than any creed. I was invited to speak to this gathering of many traditions, to offer words of wisdom for the journey that remains. Our future is in the faces I saw tonight, good people of every faith willing to risk a life together rather than apart, willing to be a person rather than a position. God bless these bridges over the empty canyons of power. God bless the ones who listen and the ones who learn.

October 13

I flew through a storm late tonight. Our plane was surrounded by lightning and tossed by high winds. We eventually had to turn away, refuel, and try again. It took hours, but we made it. Safe now in my home I think about how often life is that way: a storm comes, we are shaken by the impact of forces we cannot control, we have to make other choices and not always the ones we would prefer, we need to refuel and try again. The deeper truth is that through these moments we have another power with us. In the storm tonight I never feared, because I knew Someone was watching over me. Storms come and go. God's grace is never ending.

October 14

S orrow is the midwife of joy. That thought came to me in a dream and now I believe I understand it. For many of us who have known the hurt that life can bring, there is a conscious desire to seek out, to create, to inhabit a place of happiness. Perhaps it is a sort of holy act of defiance, a refusal to allow grief or loss to have the last word. Perhaps it is a stubborn way to cherish life, to want happier memories to endure. Perhaps it is the grace of healing that we want to extend light into every corner of the shadows we share with so many others. Whatever the reason, many of us who have been broken find joy our heart's ambition.

October 15

I am no miracle worker, but I believe my prayers make a difference, if only because they come from a humble heart, so I turn that heart outward, I let it beat in time with each of you, and I pray the rhythm of God begin: health from illness, peace from war, love from loss, abundance from scarcity, compassion from indifference, vision from blindness, comfort from pain, hope from despair, wisdom from ignorance, humility from arrogance, justice from accusation, unity from division, kindness from cruelty, life from death. I call out the good with every beat of my heart. I call out blessing. With every beat of my heart I pray the rhythm of God.

October 16

L et us walk now beneath the shadow we name Ebola. Let us not turn away from naming it, but face the fear it strikes in us. Let us pray for all those in Africa who suffer from this illness. Let us pray for those close to home who have it. Let us pray for every caregiver and responder who works to contain the disease, Let us pray for those searching for answers to stem its spread and save human lives. Ebola is a fear, but every fear falls before the power of God. Prayer is courage spoken, and through prayer we find our strength. Come now Spirit of life and drive back the shadow. Defend your people and give them the grace of your healing.

October 17

Like a compass of the spirit, my heart turns toward the children. I ask protection for every child, from every land, of every faith, from every danger. From war, from illness, from exploitation, from poverty, from hunger, from danger: protection and safety, a strong arm to enfold them, a great shield to cover them, a gentle voice to comfort them. Let innocence be all they know, the simple joys of play, the delight of discovery, the wonder of life unfolding. Let angels watch over their sleep and walk beside them during the day. Hear this prayer, God of wisdom and mercy, and call your little ones to you, shelter them with your love.

October 19

Open these words into your life, receive them into your spirit, let them be like breathing: may the peace of God enfold you, may the grace of God uphold you, may the love of God restore you, may the wisdom of God enlighten you. You are a beloved part of God's family, a life shaped by the mind and hand of the designer of all life. Each day you awake for a reason. Each moment you share is a blessing. Rise up now to the place prepared for you. Hear the voice calling your name. Do not hold back, but step forward. Open these words into your life. They are a benediction spoken for you, an acknowledgement of who you are.

October 20

I have been writing these meditations for four years now. Day after day, morning after morning, year after year: a practice of faith unbroken, constant, focused. The exercise of a spiritual life is not a sprint to quick enlightenment, but a long distance marathon that requires stamina. There are no shortcuts to faith. Long before I began writing down these thoughts I kept my daily devotions. Long after I stop writing them down I will do the same. Day after day, until the last day comes. Be patient with yourself. Be consistent. Be willing to invest your time in eternity. What you believe is what you do, one day at a time.

October 21

Sometimes it feels like we live in a box. I have had that feeling. I bet many of you have too. Instead of living in a world full of sights and sounds, options and opportunities, we feel like we have been shut off, hemmed in, enclosed in a small space with no way to get out. Depression, anxiety, isolation: all of the emotions of the box become our reality. It is for this very reason that God is in the box opening business. Setting the captives free, releasing the prisoners. Giving a new sense of freedom and perspective to those who think they have none. Welcome back to the wide open world of love. Welcome to freedom. Use the box for a planter.

October 22

Now we come to the quiet time, when all the busy day begins to sleep beneath the silver covers of the moon, when making a living gives way to being alive, and the night calls us back to the beginning, to an older time when mystery still mattered more than money. Lay down your burden, set aside your cares, fall gently into the blanket of stars. You are not measured by what you have, but by what you dream, so dream now, dream what could be, what should be, what will be, if only we trust the quiet to tell us more than the loud voices of our waking, the sounds that say so much less than silence.

October 23

I will not let this world of ours spin out of control. Even though I am only one frail life among so many, even if I have no authority other than faith, even if I stand alone against a tide greater than all the seas combined: I will remain steadfast in my witness to peace and declare that I will not let this world spin out of control. We have seen too much of fear and violence, too much of war and pain. The forces that drive the darkness will not prevail against the strength of light. Join me in believing we can do this one thing: we can alter the course of our history through the power of love. Though we are small, our witness is great, when we stand together.

October 24

Be lifted up by love, whatever your moment in life may be, be lifted up by love, the presence of love all around you, the memory of love past, the hope of love to come, the love you can see so clearly in the eyes of those who care for you, the love radiated like sunshine from children when they look at you, the small glow of love from happy couples passing by, the deep love of elders watching the world with wisdom. Open the wings of your spirit, be lifted up by love like an unseen current of air, carried over your worries, brought to a higher place, sustained in all that you do, by the love that surrounds you, the love that dwells within you, the love that is who you are and will always be.

October 26

I was sitting in a banquet, supporting a cause I have been upholding for most of my adult life, when an after dinner speaker said that one of the roadblocks we face are the people who believe in a mythical being in the sky that gives them the right to oppress others. Many people in the room clapped. At my table we were polite, like others attending who were members of a religious tradition, but the comment stung. Religion is seen as a force for intolerance. It is seen as oppressive. Not by all, but by many. Even by friends. How does my faith tell me to respond? It tells me not to be insulted but inspired: to keep building bridges, not walls.

October 27

How peaceful is my heart when I think of you, how still my mind of any worry. In these windows of prayer many images pass before me, portraits sketched by an unseen hand, of things long past and things to come, fleeting glimpses of outcomes I could not clearly imagine. But when my words turn to you, to ask for any blessing needed, the vision I see is as calm as quiet water on a windless day, a serenity of the spirit that rests undisturbed, as if the voice of heaven had caused even the waves to sleep. You are safe in the hand of God, held within the embrace eternal, as much at peace as peace may ever be.

October 28

Let there be light, please God, in all that I say and do. There are enough shadows in the world, let me not add to the darkness, but shine forth a brighter hope. Even if I am burdened in my own life, let me speak of my reality truthfully, but never slide into a constant complaint. Keep me from bitter words, a need to blame, a lament that allows no room for others. Balance my life with laughter, open my spirit to see reason to rejoice, bless me with the gift of finding the good. No matter what course my life has taken, however hard the road may have been, let me make my final journey, not in resignation, but walking to meet you with a smile.

October 29

What do you need most in your life? What blessing could make all the difference? Answer these questions in your own heart, call up the answers from deep within and let them rest in silence on the horizon of your hope. I will join you in a prayer that what you need will come to you, slowly but surely, like sunrise, like a new life awakening, a whisper becoming a song, an affirmation of all you have believed. Let our two voices echo the same appeal: please God let it be. I will wait with you to see how it may come to pass, in ways expected or unimagined, an answer of grace, a blessing needed, fulfilled at last. Please God let it be.

October 30

Here are ten playful, but perhaps poignant, spiritual oxymorons to get us thinking. An oxymoron is a combination of two words that seem to negate one another, like jumbo shrimp. (1) conditional love, (2) holy war, (3) anxious peace, (4) restricted communion, (5) my God, (6) limited grace, (7) hidden revelation, (8) fearful faith, (9) personal Savior, (10) truth claim. Can you think of others? Like Zen koans, meditating on these strange combinations of words can open doors to new insights. So please accept the ones I share with a curious spirit and see if they call you to a deeper exploration of what you have come to believe.

October 31

If I have gained any spiritual maturity in my life, I think it is reflected in some of the ways I try to live my religious life. I am secure enough in my faith to be open minded about the faith of others. I am curious to learn more and never anxious about encountering an idea that seems contrary to what I hold true. I laugh a lot. I still find myself standing under starry skies, wondering what is out there. I believe everything in creation is holy. I respect all living things and am grateful for what they have to teach me. I hope to never stop studying. I am old enough in my faith to be young at heart. I see God in you and pray you see God in me too.

NOVEMBER

November 2

Long ago my people practiced communal burial. We thought it would be a lonely thing to bury a person alone, so we gathered the bones of our loved ones and buried them together. In this way the bonds of love were unbroken. A person was never outside of community. We were born in community, lived in community, and not even death could remove us from our community. Family was the strength of the people, the sacred way of life. Kinship continued forever. This time of year I always remember that. Those we love are never lost to us. They are here, now, living their lives in a new way. The bonds of love are unbroken.

November 3

You will find your way. Never doubt that because the evidence of your resilient spirit is clear in the path you have already followed, through so many twists and turns, so many hard choices and joyful surprises, through so much of what we call life. You are a finder of trails, a watcher of signs, a carrier of wisdom, all the ancient skills that help the soul survive with what we call vision. You have traveled this far because you have trusted, because you have had faith in something greater than yourself, in a goodness and a grace that never fails, a presence stronger than change, a companion unseen but certain that we call God.

November 4

Now is sacred time. What is past may be a holy memory and what is to come may be a holy promise, but what is now is where we meet God. God dwells here, in the present, active and ever creating, moving through the Spirit, defining reality, shaping reality, available to work with us on any project that we may offer up as being worthy. Now is sacred because it is the instant of change, of decision, of birth. We take the past and bend it to the future in the now. We redeem, heal, and sanctify in the now. Look back for wisdom, look forward for dreams, but stand with God in the now and receive the authority to grow.

November 5

Give me the quiet hours, the hours when I imagine all the world is asleep, all but me, and the angels who hover nearby, watching as they always do, but never speaking, silent watchers on a silent night, sharing the night watch with me as the moon glides over the star salted sky, in the quiet hours, when prayers can be heard more clearly and memories appear in the candlelight, then I know the sleepless Spirit will soon pass by on her endless rounds, gathering up hopes like flowers, to carry them to heaven on high and sort them according to our need, making them ready, in the stillness of the night, to turn to blessings with the dawn.

November 6

I believe in goodness as the ground of being. I believe in kindness as a way of life. I believe the poor are my partners in change, the hungry are my personal responsibility, the homeless are my relatives. I believe hope is stronger than fear, truth more enduring than lies, love more powerful than force. I believe there is a calling for every person, a vocation she is invited to fulfill, a purpose only he can realize. I believe in the sanctity of compassion, the blessing of simply showing up. I believe in the right to courageous tears and the empowerment of divine laughter. I believe in you. I believe in us. I believe to believe is why we live.

November 7

The shortest distance between two points is not always the best one to take. Easy street is sometimes a dead end. If the journey is to have integrity, it is by definition going to have some steep climbs. Imagination requires risk and risk does not always pay off. Backing up and starting again is the dance of change, it is the price we pay for the discoveries we make. So do not be discouraged if your road has been a hard one, but be renewed by the fact that even if has been difficult, you have come this far, and more than that, done it with courage and conviction. The next stop is the least expected, a place of wonder worth the long walk.

November 9

There is something holy within you. I have seen it. I can testify to its presence. Even if you have been battered by a thousand storms, and felt the choices you have made have left you far from home, the light within your spirit still burns bright, so bright that on your darkest days it did not fade away. Where God has placed the dream of life there can never be a shadow. There is something holy within you, something strong and good and lasting. I celebrate the shining soul that you are, the witness to hope that you have become. I honor you for what I see beneath the surface. May your light so shine that it warms you to your core.

November 10

If I had only one prayer to ask something for myself, I think it might be for God to be with me when I make choices. So much of life is simply a matter of choice. Our reality turns on the dime of what decision we make. It is at the crossroad that we are shaped and tested, stepping off either into joy or regret. The gift of free will is the gift to choose. We make our own history with every choice we make. So I pray that when I come to a life changer of a choice that God will be with me, urging me to think deeply, keeping me in touch with my values, and staying with me after the choice is made, whatever the outcome may be.

November 11

Give us this day our daily bread, and then let us share that bread with others. It was that thought that made me think again of my own Thanksgiving tradition. It is a more Native American approach to the holiday. Rather than focusing on how much food we can accumulate and consume on that day, we express our thanks by making a special gift to the local food banks or shelters that provide for the hungry in our community. Because we are so grateful for what we have, we perform the give-away to share that blessing with as many other people as we can. We believe God is made known to us when we give bread to others.

November 12

What does God look like? That was one of my earliest spiritual questions. At age five I saw God as Grandmother, and that image has stayed with me until today. But growing up I discovered there were endless answers. Some of us prefer a father image, some want a feminine image. My friends who are Hindu say the one God can take a thousand images. My friends who are mystics say God is a spirit with no image at all. In the end, I think what we imagine should not divide us. We can agree that, just like with people, what is on the outside is not as important as what is on the inside. God looks like love because love is who God is.

November 13

As cold weather comes my mind turns to all of my spiritual neighbors, the birds of the air, the four legged creatures around me, who must live outside, no matter how bad the weather may be. Whatever I can do to make their lives easier in this season by providing food and shelter, I do so with a prayer for their safety and well-being. These creatures of God are our relatives. They are our earthly family. They have spirits as sacred as ours. Winter is our season to honor all life as life huddles together to make it through the colder days of our common existence. These short days are reminders that warmth is a gift to be shared.

November 14

I do not have much that I can offer in the things valued by this age, but I do have some timeless gifts I can share, things prized above all others by generations of my faithful ancestors. I can offer you my respect for all that you have been through, my understanding as I listen deeply to what you want to say, my support even if you stand apart from those around you, my help if you should be in need. Most of all, I can offer you my prayers, heartfelt and healing, lifting your name to a love limitless and lasting. I am not a person with much to give in worldly goods, but I am glad to give from the abundance of grace I have received and treasured.

November 16

I have been praying for one of my spiritual mentors, Thich Nhat Hanh, who is a Zen master from Vietnam. Like thousands of others around the world I discovered his writings and felt transformed by his quiet wisdom. After many years, I finally had an opportunity to see him in person. Now he is facing serious health concerns. Buddhism teaches us that all things are fleeting. It reminds us that there are realities far deeper than the worldly illusions we often inhabit. Even our heroes must pass away. But it also opens our hearts to boundless compassion. We learn when we listen. I hear the silence of Zen and smile.

November 17

B lessing counting time. Friends in the healing arts told me long ago that most people spend more time thinking and talking about what is wrong in their lives than they do in considering what is right and good in their world. So counting our blessings actually works as a counter-weight to worry. It helps hold the line against depression. Here is a start from me: for time to write, for the beauty of autumn, for piles of books, for all of my family, for this community, for all the health I have, for another day to explore, for the challenges that keep me thinking. For these and many more blessings I am grateful, dear God, so very very grateful.

November 18

G ive all that you can while you can, with whatever you have to give. Don't hold back, but throw your arms out wide, open to the sky, to the air, to the wind, and let your love billow out like streamers, colored ribbons of hope, flying out to touch all the people they can. Don't wait, don't hesitate, don't ask why, but be wild in your passion to live, to love, to give and give again, while you can, while there is still time. You are not here to be a museum, but a carnival, a happening of life, a brilliant piece of music played by the instruments of joy. Don't wait, give all that you can while you can, and do it with your eyes wide open.

November 19

I would like to honor the most courageous among us, the ones whose bravery in the face of adversity is exemplary. There are so many. I can only name a few, but I believe you will join me in celebrating them all. I honor our elders who live with physical challenges and often cope with loneliness. I honor all persons who face chronic illness or terminal illness. I honor every man or woman who gets up to go to a hard job for the sake of their family. I honor young people who try to do the right thing no matter what their friends think or say. All of these, and many more, are the quiet heroes whose courage deserves our respect and support.

November 20

There are no bars between you and the wide fields beyond. No matter how circumstance has tried to convince you that your reality is set in stone, no matter how long the same patterns have encircled you like shadows, you are free in your spirit, free enough to cross over the threshold of chance, free enough to find the friends who love you, free to be the beloved of the One who watches you each night and longs to take you flying. Step out of your own past, for it is old with worn reasons, and walk out to the gate that stands open in the garden, for your life is new with the possibilities you have already imagined.

November 21

Striving to live a spiritual life is not easy, but it is simple. Speak kindly about others, especially those with whom you disagree. Give to help those in need with both generosity and consistency. Watch for the unexpected wisdom spoken in word and deed. Carry no prejudice toward any member of your human family. Think of yourself as a healer and act accordingly. Listen more than you speak. Look for the treasure of humor and share it freely. Ask always in prayer to do what is most pleasing to God. Consider every life to be of value. Respect elders, honor youth, cherish children. Be the peace for which you live each day.

November 23

I am on the night shift of prayer, watching out for all those who may be frantic to have fun, or so far from fun they cannot remember how it feels to sleep, the late hour broken hearts, afraid to rest for fear of the memories, the graveyard shift, workers who keep going while the rest of the world sleeps, the firefighters and the cops, the nurses and the waitresses, the invisible ones beneath the overpass lying on cardboard, the endless vigil keepers waiting for news, the hospital crew and the truck drivers, I am praying for them, awake to them, remembering them, sending out love to them, until the morning brings them home.

November 24

This day was made for you, crafted by loving hands from the finest ingredients of life, the beauty of dawn rising over the edge of time, the movement of the air through the trees, the sounds of children laughing around the corner, the smiles of strangers given as a fleeting signal of our shared journey, all of these things and a thousand more, waiting for you, made for you, as you wake to walk the way prepared for you from before the first breath, sprinkled with surprises, flavored by hope, open to what you will choose to do, alive with your life, your ideas, your words that will turn the hands of history and write love with lasting letters.

November 25

I cannot tell you how many times God has lifted me up, picked me up, pulled me up when I had fallen and was as close to broken as any shattered dream can be. Therefore, my faith is not grounded in the seamless life of a person blessed from the beginning and sheltered by walls of comfort. I do not believe because I learned to do so in a classroom or a cloister. Like many of you, I have faith because I am a survivor, because I know God was there when I needed help the most, because I have been redeemed and loved and healed and set free. It is experience that brings me to pray. I am a second chance soul and grateful for it.

November 26

Notes To Self: Quirky Is Good. Talk Less, Do More. When You Say You Are Sorry, Mean It. Forgiveness Is Freedom. A Walk A Day Keeps The Doctor Away. Get Organized, Eventually. There Is A Reason For Everything. There Is An Excuse For Everything Too. Laugh A Little More. Tell Kids How Smart They Are. Say Thank You As Often As You Can. If You Have Not Learned Something New Today You Have Probably Been Sleeping. Complain To God, Not To Others. Silence Is A Vacation You Can Take Anytime. Say I Love You Daily. Be Mindful Of The Small Things, Be Patient With The Big Things. Ask Why.

November 27

I am thankful that you are part of my life, all of you who are part of our Facebook community. As we approach 7,000 members we become one of the largest inter-faith communities to meet on a daily basis in the world. And that does not include the thousands more who join us when we share the meditations, books, and prayers that welcome anyone to be part of our daily devotions. There is no way now to count how many of us there are, but each day we continue to grow. So I give thanks to God, to the Spirit, for making this happen. As I have said before, I write the words, but I am not the Author. God bless you all.

November 28

Let me share a simple truth as clearly as I can: you are loved. That is the beginning point. That is the foundation. Start by believing that you are loved, deeply loved. Before you spin out prayers for others, take on the good works you feel called to do, face the great issues that seem to confront you, just stop, stand still, breathe in, and know to the core of your being that you are loved. Stay in that moment. Let the reality of love's embrace enfold you. You are loved and deeply loved, loved forever, loved without condition, loved for who you are. Your life begins in an endless miracle. You are loved. That is the simple truth.

November 30

Something wonderful is coming this way. Each year at this time, when the ancient calendar turns, and the crisp wind blows, I feel the satin-winged angels flying through the star sprinkled night, to herald the advent of a new beginning. That is what I claim for our lives: that new beginning, that sacred start to a life renewed. Something wonderful is coming to you, to me, to all the world. No hurt or harm can hold back the healing: they must give way, yield to the power of mercy, and let the angelic chorus fill the sky with songs of hope, singing for you, singing for me, singing for the sheer joy of singing. Something wonderful is coming this way.

DECEMBER

December 1

I am open for business, the business of faith. My mind is open to think in new ways about old ideas, to explore other options, to listen to how it looks from a point of view I never even imagined. My heart is open to people of every walk of life, to all cultures and conditions, to the ones who seem like family and to the ones who seem like strangers. My spirit is open to being challenged by love to do more, to growing in wisdom and compassion, to finding myself among new friends along pathways that have no easy maps to follow. Because I have faith, because I want to serve, because I am about the business of healing: I am open, open to God.

December 2

Stand firm against the winter wind, whether of age or illness, struggle or loss, grief or lack, do not bend or break, but be lifted up, held up, made strong by the power of love that surrounds you. You are safe within the walls of hope. You are sheltered by the strength of goodness. It is the hand, the very hand of God, that holds you. It is the will of God that you be brought to quiet harbor once your storm has passed. Do not be anxious or afraid. Do not look into the long night and fear you will find no answer, but look out to the flags flying around you, the host of angels that guard you night and day. Stand firm and let faith find you.

December 3

Each year around this time, when holiday images surround us on streets and in shops, I pause to share a word with anyone who is struggling with the season. I do this not to rain on the parade, but to make certain no one is left out of the embrace of compassion that is at the real heart of our celebration. For some of us, this is a difficult anniversary, a reminder of separation, a sense of isolation. I know because I have been there. So if this is true for you, or someone you know, here is a quiet word from the heart: the light of this season is not all around you, but within you. Others may not see it, but there is always Someone who does.

December 4

There is no reason we should not sing. Standing here, among all the broken pieces of what we expected, what we thought should have happened, the way it was supposed to be, here in the empty places of our lives, here in the shadow of our own mortality, looking out into the unseen tomorrow. There is no reason we should not sing, and keep singing, until the flowers start to grow, until the mind begins to clear, until the heart of a thousand children beats ever so much stronger, and the angels in far off heaven stop and smile, thinking: they are at it again, they are still singing, all will be well, as long as they can keep singing.

December 5

I think one of the most important spiritual gifts we have is curiosity. I know there are some people who believe that faith is rock solid belief, the notion that we have all the information and ideas we will ever need. There are religious traditions that press the point and discourage questions from the floor. But faith without questions is just memorization. I feel that a curious mind is one of the greatest blessings we have as humans. I find myself in that wow-isn't-that-interesting moment on a daily basis. What does it mean? How does that work? Is that true? If we are made in the image of God, I think that image looks a lot like curiosity.

December 7

As dawn comes quietly into the world, so too will grace follow without a sound. Angels carrying blessings walk in silent procession, going about their task without speaking. The hush of birds when they pass, the calming of the wind, all testify to the reverence life pays to the healing of the One who made us all. This river of grace moves out into the world, through sleeping streets, into troubled homes, down hospital corridors, all unseen but strangely felt, as if a breeze had been moving the papers on a desk. The angels of blessing pour out hope and strength on those who have a longing heart, then rise on sunlight, to make the journey home.

December 8

May you be inspired. That alone would be a wonderful gift to receive this season. That simple and sudden moment of pure inspiration. An answer, an insight, a vision, an awakening in the Spirit that sends tingles down your back and opens your eyes to distant horizons you never even imagined. We are all in need of those crystal encounters, when it all becomes clear, when it makes sense, when we discover what we need most to understand. So let me turn my prayer wheel for you, a request that you be inspired, touched by the energy of a holy thought.

December 9

Last night at a book signing I met some people who came from different places, with different stories, who believed in different ways, and I was so glad to meet each one of them, to laugh and listen, to see the energy of their faith, the freshness of their hope, the depth of their commitment. There are more of us than we know. More of us out there who care, who believe, who are willing to celebrate difference to discover tomorrow. More of us who have not given up, who like to smile, who are willing to work to make the world a place of peace. There are more of us than we know, more of us to share the light of difference in the shadows of same.

December 10

Because I have been involved in the environmental movement for a long time, I have come to think a lot about my carbon footprint. How big of an impact am I making on the Earth by my style of living? But this made me think about my caring footprint. How much of an impact am I making in the lives of other people? I want the first one to be small. I want the second one to be as big as I can make it. So I am encouraging all of us to look behind us in a spiritual way. Is our negative impact of the planet getting smaller while our positive impact on people is getting larger? If not, we may not be walking in a balanced way.

December 11

Your hurt is my hurt, your happiness is my happiness, your gain is my gain, your loss is my loss. No we are not the same, but we are joined at the hip of the soul, bonded by the common threads of our common humanity. You may see the world spin the other way round from me, you may not hear the music I hear or wear the colors that I choose in life or death, but your breath is my breath, your heart is my heart. We are siblings of the soul, made of common clay from a common hand, created to inherit the call of love that stirs our common spirit. Your mind is not my mind, but your life is my life, our fate as common as the sky we share.

December 12

Thank you for all that you have sacrificed for the sake of others. Thank you for never being afraid to try. Thank you for the quiet way you have worked so hard for so long for so little for so many. Thank you for standing up for what you believed even though it cost you more than you ever let on. Thank you for being true to your vision even when others told you to give up and come home to their small definition of who you were supposed to be. Thank you for the laughter and the listening, so freely shared when they were needed most. Thank you for being an inspiration without even knowing it. And yes, I really am writing these words just for you.

December 14

It shall not be so among you, all of you, who seek to walk in a sacred way, to fail to forgive, to be quick to blame, to look the other way, but rather that you hold together, through every time of struggle, loving one another as you have been loved, respecting your differences, valuing your opposites, seeing strength in change, until you have learned, discovered, the community you were designed to be, called to be, by the author of all your fates, the focus of every prayer, the holy source of who you are, and when that happens, as it will happen, peace will fall down like snow, hope like spring blossoms, grace like stars on a clear night.

December 15

Among the Aboriginal People there is the tradition of the walkabout, an intentional time when young persons go out in search of themselves in the Outback, the remote places of interior Australia. I think there are times when we all could benefit from taking a walkabout of the soul, times when we let our spirits roam free, out into the wilder places remote from our comfortable dogma. We need the new. We grow in the strange. We learn from the challenge. God is not always found in the tame spaces, but in the outback of faith. So I think I will wander into the welcoming wilderness, looking to discover what waits beyond my own horizon.

December 16

Hand me what is heaviest for you to carry, for I have broad shoulders of faith and strength of prayer enough for us both, until we reach a quiet place beside the run of time, where you can rest beneath a sun calmed sky. Hand me your greatest burden, for I have energy to spare on this long walk home, and many stories left to tell, until we reach the hearth of welcome, the shelter of all spirit faring souls, where you will sleep away your cares in still rooms of serenity. Hand me your deepest question, and while you dream I will lift it to heaven, trusting for an answer, an answer you will know when you wake.

December 17

I had a happy memory come back to me, unexpectedly, just rising up like an old friend from long ago. It was the memory of one of my favorite toys as a child, a much loved, much used source of simple joy. The memory made me smile. And it made me think: how often our unhappy memories walk in on us like they own the place. They don't call ahead. They don't even knock. They just show up. But the happy memories are more polite. They wait for us to invite them back. So I have decided to be much more intentional in my remembering. I will consciously recall a reason to smile, once a day. I hope you will join me. Happy memories.

December 18

I come from those they call the salt of the earth, the common, everyday, hardworking, honest people they call the salt of the earth. The irony is that when this description was first made salt was anything but common. Salt was rare and precious. Soldiers in those ancient days were paid in salt. It was like gold. So to refer to the common people as salt was to call them precious, to say that they were of great value. As it was then so it is now, even if we have salt at every table. People are still of great value. The most humble person is of great value. Every life is precious in the eyes of God. What is common is rare. What is everyday is eternal.

December 19

Let me speak with words as clear as I can: we are the people of now. That is how God made us. That is the great secret of our existence, a truth right before us. We are not the people of long ago, though we may try to push ourselves through tradition, to be our past and claim it can never change. We are not disembodied from this time to live in worlds we only think, but never see or feel. We are the people of now, the keepers of this moment, this choice, this single act. For on what we choose to do, what we hold sacred, what we claim or release, is made the only life we will ever know this side of paradise. We are the people of now.

December 21

I had to give up something I really wanted this month. It may seem small to others, but my annual attendance at the Nutcracker ballet has meant a lot to me. The joyful music and movement of that great dance lift my spirits. But this year I had to miss it and that has gotten me to thinking, thinking about how much of our lives are lived by this same rhythm, the rhythm of giving and receiving, having and letting go, laughing and longing. As human beings we are not watching the dance, but living it, forever moving between our hopes and fears, our dreams and reality. If you are feeling the sweet but sad this season, you are not alone. Many are dancing beside you.

December 22

A long night brings me to find dawn already on my doorstep, my old friend of light waiting at my window, and the family of flyers that I feed already gathered in the garden. How simple is the passage of our lives, from one vision to the next, one prayer to the next, it all happens so seamlessly, no matter what we carry with us, how heavy our footsteps from one room to another, time glides past us to open the door. I send out blessings to a world busy with being, asking grace to find those like me, the dreamers who do not sleep, the keepers who give away, the curious without a question. Be at peace today. Be blessed in every way.

December 23

It is not for me to tell you who you are, but please let me share this small insight. The beauty of your life is contained in its simplicity. You were born to be an agent of grace, sharing kindness into the world. You are an unconscious healer, restoring hope into the world. These two simple definitions are a spiritual job description. They represent the core of your calling. I believe they describe all of us, uniting us into a shared purpose. Beyond all of the differences we construct among ourselves, we have a common task. Agents of grace. Sources of hope. If we see ourselves in this way, the complexity we imagine becomes the simplicity we are.

December 24

We are on the threshold now, standing just a step away from the light, with all the things we dreamed so near at hand, it seems like a different world from the one we thought we knew. Love is like that. It transforms. It enlightens. It makes whole. Love is there, right there, waiting for us to discover it and release its power into the lives of countless people, people who will be restored before they even know it, lifted up before they can even believe it, swept into tomorrow with the joy of a holy promise fulfilled. We are on the threshold now, ready to step over, cross over into a time of peace, a hope so strong it casts out every shadow, now and forever.

December 25

On this holy night, when hope is newborn into the world, we are all called together, beneath the star we see, beneath the angels we hear, to stand with creation in the common straw of our fragile lives, and behold the miracle of a God who cares. In an age of fear when religion can be more of a weapon than a blessing, this small infant sleeping in the arms of a poor girl from the back country is the last place many might look for an answer, but it is the first place we should turn to discover the power of love. How blessed we are, however we pray, to be the sons and daughters of the child who is older than heaven itself.

December 26

Today is Boxing Day, an oddly named post-holiday moment when the upper class used to give boxes of gifts to their lower class workers. I know people today mark the day in different ways than that, but for me it is an opportunity to pause and reflect on this idea of "class" in our world. The economic measuring stick is still very much a reality in global culture. The Have's. The Have Nots. If the glow of Christmas is to have any lasting meaning, surely it is to cast a light of equality around us all. So on this Boxing Day let us all renew our shared pledge to economic justice and the right to dignity for every human being.

December 28

Walk the sacred way of your own heart, following where you believe you are led. Do not imagine that you are the first to pass this way, or that you have made the path for yourself. Have the humility to see the trail before you, even if the signs for it are few and far between. Remain true to where it takes you, even though it may be a steep climb. Do not fear that you will lose your direction, but be trusting in the holy guide that shows you where to turn. If you meet another walk together as long as you can, but if you walk alone then go in love for any who may follow. Stop to rest as often as you can and notice what is around you. Travel well, walk in peace. .

December 29

I am giving serious consideration to declaring today National Dreamers Day. I think we are long overdue for this kind of recognition, especially since we have done much more for the world than most important people, and even more especially since it is getting harder and harder to find the time to do a proper job of dreaming in a world that is so busy doing something it doesn't understand the necessity of doing nothing, nothing except dreaming, imagining, wondering, thinking like driving without any particular destination in mind, just sightseeing the back roads of the brain, looking for what is around the next bend. We need a day for that.

December 30

What a deep mystery it is to be family. Those unseen instincts of love bind us to others we claim as our own. They are the most ancient of feelings, the primal urge to care that brought us out of the darkness of isolation into the light of being who we are, human creatures, made human by our willingness to share. At its best, a family is a tender miracle of belonging. At its worst it is the definition of sorrow. May God bless your family, whether it is a great tribe of souls related in every direction, or only a small band of hopeful hearts looking out into the world together. May your family be the home you seek and the haven you need for every season of your life.

December 31

There is no harm that can come to you, no matter how frail and fragile you feel, for this passing stream of light is not the measure of all you are, but only the rough canvas on which the colors of your life are forever being painted. You are not encompassed by a clock, marked off into a reality of artificial movements, but designed to be free from such constraints, able to rise up on the wings of your own imagination to see the hands behind the time. Hurt may happen, but it will never last nor have the final word in the sonnet that is your soul, for that wisdom will go on and on, speaking wonders into a future you cannot even name.